MANAGING IN A GLOBAL ORGANIZATION
Keys to Success in a Changing World

Carol Kinsey Goman, Ph.D.

CRISP PUBLICATIONS, INC.
Menlo Park, California

MANAGING IN A GLOBAL ORGANIZATION
Keys to Success in a Changing World

Carol Kinsey Goman, Ph. D.

CREDITS
Editor: **Nancy Shotwell**
Managing Editor: **Kathleen Barcos**
Typesetting: **ExecuStaff**
Cover Design: **Barbara Ravizza**

Copyright © 1994 by Crisp Publications, Inc.

Printed in the United States of America

English language Crisp books are distributed worldwide. Our major international distributors include:

CANADA: Reid Publishing Ltd., Box 69559-109 Thomas St., Oakville, Ontario Canada L6J 7R4. TEL: (416) 842-4428, FAX: (416) 842-9327

AUSTRALIA: Career Builders, P. O. Box 1051, Springwood, Brisbane, Queensland, Australia, 4127. TEL: 841-1061, FAX: 841-1580

NEW ZEALAND: Career Builders, P. O. Box 571, Manurewa, Auckland, New Zealand. TEL: 266-5276, FAX: 266-4152

JAPAN: Phoenix Associates Co., Mizuho Bldg. 2-12-2, Kami Osaki, Shinagawa-Ku, Tokyo 141, Japan. TEL: 3-443-7231, FAX: 3-443-7640

Selected Crisp titles are also available in other languages. Contact International Rights Manager Suzanne Kelly at (415) 323-6100 for more information.

Library of Congress Catalog Card Number 93-73183
Goman, Carol Kinsey
Managing in a Global Organization
ISBN 1-56052-268-2

This book is printed on recyclable paper with soy ink.

Dedication

*To Joyce Turley Nicholas—friend, international speaker
and traveler extraordinaire—who generously initiated and supported
my own international speaking career.*

and

*To my husband, Ray K. Goman—whose first reaction to one of my trips
is to list all the reasons why he can't possibly go along—but once he does,
dives right into the local action and dines on sea blubber in Hong Kong,
bobs around the inland passage in a rowboat to tow a small glacier
for ice carving, and goes bungy-jumping in New Zealand.*

I can't thank both of you enough.

INTRODUCTION

The era of globalization is at hand. Whether you work for a multinational organization or manage a small business, you are competing with other workers, products, services and ideas from around the world. To survive and prosper in today's business environment, we all must think globally.

Some industries have already felt the impact of globalization. If you are in one of these fields—telecommunications, electronic/computer, finance, pharmaceutical, oil, chemical, transportation or automotive industries—you live with the daily reality of multicultural, international business. If not—get ready—it's just a matter of time.

Managing in a Global Organization is a compilation of surveys, research and personal international experience in an area of study—human behavior—that is always fascinating and challenging. The book is divided into eight chapters. The first chapter, "Globalization," outlines the effect of the worldwide marketplace on business today. The second chapter, "The Global Organization," defines the organizational corporate structure and looks at the creation of a global culture. Chapter three discusses the roles and responsibilities of management in leading employees into a globalized work environment. Chapter four, "Managing Change," looks at change as an anticipated, continuous process within the global organization, and challenges managers to upgrade change-management skills. The fifth chapter discusses the intricacies of doing business internationally, and offers suggestions for preparation. "Global Communication," the sixth chapter, highlights the special challenges of communicating across borders. Chapter seven looks at the international assignment and outlines the requirements for successful overseas relocations.

Chapter eight, "Resources for Global Managers," offers the reader an excellent reference section with detailed information on:

○ International business organizations

○ Directories for global business resources

○ Government agencies that aid international business

O Books and tapes for supplementary information

O Universities with international business programs

Throughout the book I use certain terms which the purist (rightly so) might object to. With apologies to other residents in North and South America, I use the word "Americans" to refer to citizens of the United States. I interchange the terms "international" organization, "multinational" organization and "global" organization to refer to the same thing. I define the word "expatriate," in its contemporary usage by Americans abroad and personnel administrators here, to apply to any United States citizens who live outside their own country. And I use the term "global managers" to encompass anyone whose responsibilities require them to deal with people and human culture in today's business environment.

I would like to acknowledge all the international managers whom I interviewed in preparation for this book. Without their participation I would have plenty of facts . . . but far fewer stories and examples.

I also want to thank my stepdaughter, Jennifer Goman, general manager for the San Diego World Trade Association. She initiated the chapter on global resources and was a continual source of information and support.

MANAGING IN A GLOBAL ORGANIZATION

Keys to Success in a Changing World

CONTENTS

CONTENTS (continued)

CONTENTS (continued)

C H A P T E R

1

Globalization

"For all practical purposes, all business today is global. Those individual businesses, firms, industries, and whole societies that clearly understand the new rules of doing business in a world economy will prosper; those that do not will perish."

—Ian Mitroff, Professor
University of Southern California

"... in order to capitalize on the globalization of commerce ... American managers will have to think beyond the borders of the United States."

—John S. McClenhen,
Senior International Editor, *Industry Week*

WHAT IS GLOBALIZATION?

Globalization has become a byword of the 1990s. Political, economic and social changes are restructuring the world. Recent advances in telecommunication technology connects countries as readily as next-door neighbors. Markets no longer stop at national boundaries; neither do corporate operations. Long-standing geographic, regulatory and industry barriers are coming down, and a truly global marketplace is emerging.

For organizations to flourish, let alone survive, in the decade of the 1990s, their perspective must be global. To respond to the global challenge, we have to understand the nature of the global forces affecting us as well as the impact that these forces have on business strategy development. Also, we must, if possible, anticipate the interaction between globalization and corporate organizational structures.

3

Globalization is an attitude—a way of thinking of the world as a unified market-place rather than a collection of national markets. We must be constantly looking for solutions to maintaining competitiveness in the face of forces that continue to transform the global marketplace. Globalization is a business strategy—a plan to develop and transfer innovations to subsidiaries around the world, to compete and collaborate internationally, and to manage independent multinational operations coordinated by a global mission. The global organization looks for ways to maintain national responsiveness and global integration at the same time. Globalization is a management challenge—a process that includes building worldwide teams, customizing products and services to diverse national preferences, communicating to a multinational workforce, and developing career strategies with a global view.

GLOBALIZATION AS A MATTER OF SURVIVAL

Prior to World War II, the number of American firms involved in foreign direct investment was relatively small. Even after the war, the United States was still focused mainly on its domestic market—which provided an unsurpassed strength and competitive advantage. While the U. S. was producing unique products and offering them almost exclusively to an internal market, we faced little international competition. When we exported those same products, it was without alterations or sensitivity to cultural differences.

Without the buffer of a strong domestic market, much of the rest of the industrialized world was forced to learn how to compete internationally. Faced with accelerated global competition, the 1980s showed us that, with a few exceptions, American companies weren't as good as our foreign competitors who had practice playing the global game. We didn't produce quality products. Our customer service was lacking. We were too slow in responding to international needs and in bringing new products to market. The Japanese and some of our other foreign competitors were beating us because they were better—offering higher quality, better customer service and faster innovation. The result is that most American companies are still trying to catch up to the training and experience of our international competitors.

At a recent conference on world trade in Southern California, Gerald Schleif, president of WD-40, opened his address with the following comment: "U.S. companies are neophytes in the global game compared to the Japanese, the English, the Dutch and the Middle Easterners. We've got a lot of catching up to do. It's been their playground for years."

The world has clearly entered an era of unprecedented global economic activity, including worldwide production, distribution and global strategic alliances. The majority of the world's largest corporations now perform an increasing proportion of their business activities outside their national borders. A host of major multinational corporations have more than half their sales in foreign markets rather than at their home base of operations (e.g., the U.S.-based IBM, Dow Chemical, Coca Cola and Colgate-Palmolive, the Switzerland-based Nestlè and Ciba-Geigy, the Ireland-based Jefferson Smurfit group, the Netherlands-based Philips, the Sweden-based Volvo and Electrolux, Japan's Sony and Honda, and France's Michelin, to name just a few in a long list.)

We have to get used to the fact that we are no longer economically self-sufficient or capable of commercial isolation. International commerce is vital to American prosperity. In the United States, exports and imports have increased more than 10 times in the last two decades, and of the 1000 largest industrial companies in America, 700 expect their growth abroad to exceed their domestic growth in the next five years.

Globalization today is a matter of survival. Companies not able to adopt this new perspective will have a much harder time facing up to the new realities. To succeed, corporations must develop global strategies incorporating new approaches to managing research and development, production, marketing, finance and international human resource systems.

Managing with a global perspective and modern business management are becoming synonymous. Organizations that still don't recognize a globalized business environment (or those who recognize it but underestimate the effect of doing business in a globalized environment) will see their profits and jobs disappear.

A CASE IN POINT

Frank A. Shrontz, chairman of Boeing, is pushing his top 15,000 white-collar workers through a course in "world-class competitiveness." A 384-page course manual begins with this from Mr. Shrontz: "During the past decade or so, we've seen a number of great American industries surrender their leadership to competitors abroad. It would be tragic if we allowed the same fate to strike the U.S. aerospace industry."

Some companies are investing in university programs to educate global managers. The Estēe Lauder firm contributed $10 million toward this goal at the University of Pennsylvania to establish an Institute of Management and International Studies. Their president, Leonard Lauser, stated bluntly that unless American management can learn to compete on a global scale, the country's position as a major industrial power will decline.

GLOBAL FORCES

There are four major advancing globalization forces: economic growth, technological advances, the shifting of traditional power structures, and accelerating global competition.

Economic Growth Today's global economy is poised for extraordinary expansion in the 1990s and beyond. Changing social, economic and demographic patterns—regional, national and global—are leading to the emergence of many new markets.

Economic growth has shifted from its traditional areas of concentration in the industrialized countries of the northern hemisphere. Newly industrialized countries of the Far East have many followers all over the world. Labor-intensive manufacturing jobs continue to migrate to low wage countries. The shifting pattern of economic dynamism in developing countries increasingly represents a tremendous market opportunity.

The world shrinks every day. The corporate segments of the economies of North America, Europe and Asia are becoming internationalized at an increasing rate. Nations are more economically intertwined. About

$1 trillion in annual sales is generated today by foreign operations of U.S. companies. That's four times the value of exports made in the United States. One out of six United States manufacturing jobs is dependent on foreign trade, while four out of five new manufacturing jobs result from international commerce.

Technological Advances   According to John Naisbett, author of *Megatrends*, "Two recent inventions have played the key role in transforming the planet into a global economic village: the jet airplane and the communication satellite. The former—the jet airplane—has enabled some 2,000,000 passengers to take off from 16,000 airports on 650 domestic and international airlines toward thousands of destinations all over the globe on an average day. The latter—the communication satellite—has helped to collapse the information float, enabling the world to share information almost instantaneously."

To a large extent, globalization is technology driven—or, at least, technology dependent. The increasingly freer flow of goods, information, ideas, capital and people across national frontiers links the countries of the world as never before.

There have been tremendous advances in the ability to communicate globally. Fax machines, computer modems and the previously mentioned satellites permit offices worldwide to exchange information more easily than could have been done a decade ago by offices across town. "Info-space" is the term used to describe information that is dispersed at the same time all around the globe. Technology allows us to communicate globally, quickly, meaningfully, accurately.

Shifting Power Structures   The ongoing economic and social unification of the world's community is supplemented by the fragmentation of traditional political structures and the emergence of new centers of international influence. Gradually, national governments are being forced, through economic necessity, to give up parts of their control. A new world order is emerging: the triad of the European Community, the North American trading block, and a Japan-led Asian-Pacific alliance.

Increasing Competition   To date, we in North America have seen only the beginning of international competition. In the future, businesses will be pressured even more by world-class competition from all over the globe. Gary Markovits, patent process program manager at IBM's Research and General Technology divisions, says: "If you look ahead five to ten years you can expect to see very large numbers of manufacturers capable of doing world-class manufacturing and marketing. That means they've conquered the quality issues, they've conquered the manufacturing and they're capable of marketing anywhere in the world."

Organizations in the United States have no choice but to adapt to these driving forces. There is no alternative but to substantially alter the ways in which we think about the global marketplace and the ways in which we get work done. While this takes fundamental structural shifts in our organizations, we simply have no alternative. The rest of the world will change without us if we do not change fast enough. For the North American work force, it is an emotionally wrenching reality that such massive organizational restructuring results in some jobs disappearing forever, while others open in new areas—requiring entirely new skills. But we are left with few other options. We are competing with companies and with workers (both unskilled and highly skilled) from around the world. Revolutionary change is occurring in American business because American business has to change to survive.

THE WIDE, WIDE WORLD OF WORKERS

A fundamental shift is underway in how and where the world's work gets done. The key to this change is the emergence of a truly global labor force, talented and capable of accomplishing just about anything, anywhere. *Fortune* recently quoted Larry Irving, an executive of Daniel Industries who moved from Houston to run a factory that his company bought in eastern Germany: "The average American doesn't realize that there is a truly competitive work force out there that is vying for their jobs. The rest of the world is catching up."

If an average American worker doesn't realize there's a global labor market, the average multinational organization certainly does. One international business consultant advises corporations to "think in terms of a 150-hour work week spread out over fourteen time zones—constantly online."

Interviews with executives around the globe reveal that sophisticated work is being parceled out to faraway nations whose labor forces are exceedingly capable. A top executive at Seimens, the giant German industrial and electronics company, says: "Thirty years ago they could barely spell 'steam turbine' in India. Now we are building the biggest ones in the world there."

On a recent trip to Ireland, I saw dozens of offices devoted to handling complex service work from the United States. In County Cork, 150 Metropolitan Life workers analyze medical insurance claims to determine if they are eligible for reimbursement. This function is not unsophisticated. It demands considerable knowledge of medicine, the American medical system and the insurance business.

Until recently, most of the $450 billion that America has invested in factories and offices abroad has gone to Western countries. Currently, however, the flow of money—$26 billion in 1992—is beginning to shift toward emerging countries that have skilled work forces:

○ In Bangalore, India, 3M makes tapes, chemicals and electrical parts. In the mid-eighties, Texas Instruments started setting up an impressive software programming operation also in Bangalore, partly because of the high level of talented software designers in India. Now Motorola and IBM have set up software programming offices west of Madras.

○ In Guadalajara, Mexico, Hewlett-Packard assembles computers and designs computer memory boards. Half the employees at HP's plants in Guadalajara have advanced degrees. These engineers design components that are manufactured worldwide.

○ In Jamaica 3,500 people work at office parks connected to the United States by satellite dishes. There they make airline reservations and process tickets, handle phone calls to toll-free numbers, and do data entry.

○ On Batam Island in Indonesia, more than forty companies (including AT&T, which manufactures telephones there) have set up factories in newly established industrial parks.

○ Although Motorola still does the bulk of its R&D work in the United States, the company is expanding the amount of research done in Southeast Asia after the commercial popularity of the Singaporean design and manufacturing of two Motorola pagers. AT&T Bell Laboratories already has researchers there.

WORLDWIDE EXCELLENCE

Centers of technological innovation exist around the world in various locations—research labs, universities and corporations. The idea is to have enough "geographic flexibility" to identify and harness these intellectual resources and incorporate them into a global strategy.

Many multinational organizations are relocating some functions on a global scale to places other than headquarters. The Dutch electronics company, Philips, established "Centers of Competence" in regions where national cultural values and behaviors best match the competency. For example, Philips moved their long-range planning technology from the United States to the Far East, where they could take advantage of longer-term thinking and reward patterns. In similar efforts, IBM and Digital Equipment both moved research and development centers to Italy, where innovation has been highly successful.

Banta Limited, a Canadian footwear company, has established centers of excellence throughout the world that serve the needs of the rest of the organization. Holland has become the center for research work, Indonesia provides the latest rubber footwear technology, Mexico is leading in plastic-injection molded footwear, and Europe takes the lead in various retail marketing concepts.

Other multinationals have centers in various regions to take advantage of locally developed leading practices. Otis Elevator's newest product, Elevonic-411, was developed by six research centers in five countries.

THE MOVABLE LABOR FORCE

An article in the *Harvard Business Review* addresses the fact that for more than a century, companies have moved manufacturing operations to take advantage of local labor pools. But now ". . . human capital, once considered to be the most stationary factor in production, increasingly flows across national borders as easily as cars, computer chips, and corporate bonds. Just as managers speak of world markets for products, technology, and capital, they must now think in terms of a world market for labor." The article goes on to say that the globalization of labor is good for the world as it allows human capital to be deployed where it can be used most productively. "Countries that recognize it as a positive trend and facilitate the flow of people will benefit the most."

At the highest skill levels, the labor market has been international for many years. Bell Laboratories physicists, for example, come from universities in England or India as well as from American schools. At Schering-Plough's research labs the first language of biochemists is as likely to be Hindi, Japanese or German as it is English.

As the labor market tightens and becomes even more specialized, many employers will expand the geography of their recruitment efforts. One American example was our reaction to the shortage of nurses for U.S. hospitals. As the shortage became acute, health care providers began to recruit in widening circles. What was once a local labor market became regional, then national and finally international. By the end of the 1980s, it became commonplace for New York hospitals to advertise in Dublin and Manilla for skilled nurses.

Computer programming is another example of an American industry that is hiring more skilled workers from abroad. In the computer programming industry, where projects require large temporary work crews, companies import software engineers using a visa that lets foreigners get paid in their native currencies.

Tandem Computers recently had up to fifty programmers working on a project for Lockheed Corporation. About half the workers were provided by a subcontractor which utilized both United States citizens and Indian nationals.

FOREIGN OWNERSHIP OF U.S. COMPANIES

Foreign investment poured into the United States during the 1980s, soaring 616 percent to $403 billion by the decade's end. Although the binge has leveled out, and relatively few new foreign companies are predicted to invest in the U.S. in the near future, the growth of existing ventures will continue.

Those who resisted the foreign influx feared the imminent loss of American jobs, technology and national security. But according to a recent *Trend Letter* by John Naisbitt, few of these fears materialized: "Instead, foreign-owned firms erected strategic gateways between American communities and the global marketplace. Foreign-based money, ideas and technologies created hundreds of thousands of high-skill jobs and unprecedented prosperity for dozens of U.S. communities. One in twenty Americans works for a foreign firm, earning an average of 22 percent more than the overall private work force."

SOME CASES IN POINT

With a $2.6 billion investment in Ohio, Honda built plants in the towns of Marysville, East Liberty and Anna in which more than 10,000 Americans turn out as many as 540,000 Civics and Accords a year. BMW is planning to invest $640 million in a 1.9-million-square-foot factory in South Carolina, offering jobs to some 2,000 workers. The joint venture between U.S. Steel and the Korean steel company POSCO puts over 1,000 locals to work in a facility recently modernized for $450 million in Pittsburg, California.

Nowhere is the impact of foreign-based companies felt so strongly as in the Dallas/Fort Worth area, which is among the world's top ten sites for multi-national headquarters. Foreign-based companies poured an estimated $827 million into the area's economy in just one year.

WHO IS THEM AND US?—RETHINKING ALL BOUNDARIES

Foreign ownership of companies is causing countries to become increasingly interconnected. Last year I toured a Maquiladora plant in Tijuana. The operations manager conducting the tour was an American from Arkansas, the work force was Mexican, and the company belonged to the Japanese. As my American guide described the assembly process, he said, "That's the way we do it here." All I could think of was, "Who's we?"

A CASE IN POINT

Corporation X is headquartered in the United States. Its top management, its board of directors and all of its major shareholders are United States citizens. However, most of Corporation X's employees are non-Americans. All research and development, product design and manufacturing are done in Asia, Europe and Latin America. Its laboratories and factories are located abroad.

Corporation Y is headquartered in another industrialized nation with all top managers, directors and major shareholders being citizens of that nation. Corporation Y employs an American work force. Its R&D, product design, and most of its manufacturing is done in the United States.

Who is "them" and who is "us"?

From *A Manager's Guide to Globalization* by Stephen Rhinesmith.

We are finding it more and more difficult to define what are exclusively American economic investments. Ford is building cars in Mexico, and Honda is building them in Ohio.

In his book *The Work of Nations,* Robert Reich said: "We are living through a transformation that will rearrange the politics and economies of the coming century. There will be no national products or technologies, no national corporations, no national industries. There will no longer be national economies. All that will remain rooted within national borders are the people who comprise a nation. We are becoming 'global webs' in which products are international composites."

As Dr. Reich goes on to point out, and many others have confirmed, business is being conducted on a transnational basis. Partnering across national borders has become commonplace, and even those enterprises that consider themselves purely local cannot escape the impact of globalized markets.

CHAPTER

2

The Global Organization

> *Any institution has to be organized so as to bring out the talent and capabilities within the organization; to encourage people to take initiative, give them a chance to show what they can do and a scope in which to grow.*
>
> —Peter Drucker, Author and
> Claremont Graduate Center Professor

> *Developing a global attitude must become the norm rather than the exception, regardless of the size of your organization.*
>
> —Sonja Bata, Director
> Bata Limited

THE STRUCTURE OF A GLOBAL ORGANIZATION

International business began in America before the Civil War. It is not a new concept. However, most American companies were *ethnocentric*—with centralized decision making and tight control of their foreign subsidiaries from domestic headquarters.

A
CASE
IN
POINT

Morton International began in 1848 as Morton Salt and now has four chemical groups as well as a division that manufactures air bags for the automotive industry. Although Morton has subsidiaries all over the world, the global operation is tightly controlled from headquarters in Chicago.

Other international organizations view their foreign operations as semi-autonomous. In these companies, global management is a "tight-loose" affair, with local subsidiaries making many decisions, but with centralized headquarters in control of core issues.

McDonald's Corporation prefers to call itself a "multi-local company" rather than a multinational one, because within the 65 countries in which it operates, there is local control over many issues. (For instance, at a McDonald's in Germany, as a local adaptation, customers can order beer. This beverage is not part of the menu anywhere else in the world.) At the same time, there is responsibility at McDonald's headquarters to maintain universal standards for food preparation and operations around the world.

Many globalized organizational structures are heading toward a more *polycentric* design with less headquarter authority and more decentralized interconnected facilities with greater authority and local control. These organizations are characterized by multiple entities, each with a high degree of autonomy and reciprocal interdependencies.

Parker Hannifin Corporation has subsidiaries and (a few) joint ventures within 58 countries. If you picture a hub with spokes radiating outward from the center, at its core you find headquarters in Cleveland, Ohio, but the spokes leading away from the hub represent the decentralized business units in various countries that also function with a high degree of independence and responsibility.

It is predicted that the global corporation of the future will move even more toward decentralization—with global strategies and responsibilities removed from the function of corporate headquarters to be shared by global teams of executives with greater independence and interdependence between international units. A basic management challenge will be to integrate offshore organizations into a community of international operations while maintaining local identities and loyalties.

Most international organizations initially began with a matrix approach—some executives looked after regional responsibilities and others looked after specific product lines. But today, it is difficult to control these operations in order to respond to global forces. Often the global priorities of the head office clash with the local imperatives of each subsidiary company. That is why many multinationals are now trying to establish a more globally integrated strategy, where the insular nature of subsidiaries is broken down and the gap is bridged between global and local markets.

Beyond the decentralization and the efforts made to restructure around a truly global strategy, there are some other structural trends that, individually or collectively, probably represent the future direction for most global organizations. They are as follows: 1) the continued flattening of the organizational hierarchy; 2) the realization that (when it comes to global competitiveness) bigger is not necessarily better; 3) the trend toward a "boundaryless" organization, where the contribution of employees is not restricted by job title or department; 4) the modular structure, in which companies focus on their core competencies; 5) the "virtual corporation" that encourages partner companies to band together in collaboration for a limited time to exploit a particular market opportunity.

The Flattening of the Hierarchy

In the United States, since the 19th century the hierarchy had been viewed as the most efficient structure for an organization. The leader was at the top of this "command and control" model, and most of the primary responsibilities and rewards were reserved for the upper levels of management. In a global environment, however, we are finding that to compete, we must collaborate, and organizational structures must evolve into more cooperative forms.

At the forefront in the United States, companies like General Electric and Pepsico are breaking up old hierarchical structures modeled after the military into collections of small units. Run informally, these nimble teams hand the baton of decision making to front-line factory workers and try to reproduce the energy and intensity that power small businesses.

It is predicted by most business researchers that the organizations of the future will resemble networks or modules. The successful ones will have flattened hierarchies and more cross-functional linkages. Organizational observers as diverse as futurist Alvin Toffler and author Tom Peters agree that the demise of the old authoritarian hierarchies, from the U.S.S.R. to General Motors, is a global, historical phenomenon that none can evade. The global company in the future will be flatter, leaner and more aggressive than most companies today. It will have to be that way in order to have the flexibility to respond to rapid change.

A CASE IN POINT

Nucor Steel of Charlotte, North Carolina, is an $850 million company. It has a corporate staff of seventeen and only four levels of management. The remainder of Nucor's 3,700 employees are workers.

Bigger Is Not Better

Until the mid-1980s the larger the organization, the more successful it was thought to be. Small companies wanted to get big. Big companies wanted to get bigger. The stock market rewarded growth. Conglomerates proliferated. Then, around 1985, the rules changed. We found out that traditional big companies were having a hard time competing with a lot of their smaller, more focused rivals. Big companies just weren't as flexible as their smaller counterparts. Despite some advantages of size (resources, stability, etc.), larger organizations were impaired by over-staffing, bureaucracy and too many layers of management.

The restructuring trend now in progress is driven by the competitive need to reduce the size of our organizations. It is being made possible by new technology that relays crucial information directly to workers (without the need for middle management interpretation) and allows senior executives to instantly monitor performance at the lower level.

Parker Hannifin Corporation employs 27,000 people globally, but each of its approximately 140 facilities is limited to about 250 to 300 people. Within these small plants, the chief executive officer knows all the employees, knows all the customers, and knows the competition *very well*. When a facility grows beyond the optimum number, the corporation will spin off another plant. Like many other global competitors have learned, Parker Hannifin believes that in its industry (capital equipment), bigger is not better.

Futurists predict that we will see more and more large organizations breaking up into many (even hundreds of) smaller independent business units. Matsushita Electric Industrial has 161 independent units, Hitachi Ltd. has 600 companies, Johnson and Johnson operates 106 autonomous companies, and Hewlett-Packard has 50 independent units.

The Boundaryless Organization

In the global organization there will be fewer and fewer boundaries of any kind. In the book *Control Your Destiny or Someone Else Will,* Jack Welch, General Electric's chief executive since 1981, talks about the process of "boundarylessness." Boundarylessness is Welch's term for the breaking down of barriers that divide employees—such as hierarchy, job function and geography—and distance companies from suppliers and customers. In this vision workers spring from one project to another without regard for permanent structure. At GE, that means sonar experts from the aerospace division can jump into advanced ultrasound technology in the medical systems business without bureaucratic restraint. Mr. Welch says, "I wish we'd understood sooner how much leverage you can get from the flow of ideas among all the business units."

The once very rigid and unbreachable boundaries of business are fading in the face of change. All this rapid change—instantaneous communications, a globalized marketplace, new technologies in product and production, and heightened multinational competition—has forced organizations to recognize the importance of creativity and innovation from all members of the company. Global organizations are going to need cultures that are equipped to adapt creatively to a changing environment. They must have internal processes that are creative, generative and productive rather than controlled, confining and normative. In short, we must create cultures that unshackle the human brain and exploit its productive potential.

The 1991 May–June issue of *Harvard Business Review* featured an article by Rosabeth Moss Kanter entitled "Transcending Business Boundaries: 12,000 World Managers View Change." It began: "For much of the twentieth century, business managers around the world confronted a series of walls. Walls between nations that establish the boundaries of national markets, national practices, or national, social, economic, and political systems. Walls between the company and the society in which it exists, drawing sharp distinctions between corporate interests and social interests. Walls between work and home, separating those activities that involve earning a living from those that constitute just plain living. Walls within the workplace itself, dividing managers from workers, function from function, line from staff. And walls between the company and its stake-holders, including suppliers, customers, and venture partners. Now . . . the walls are crumbling."

The Modular Structure

One new structural approach to globalization is the "modular company." In a recent *Fortune* issue, it was reported: "In a leap of industrial evolution, many companies are shunning vertical integration for a lean, nimble structure centered on what they do best. The idea is to nurture a few core activities—designing and marketing computers, copiers or autos, for example—and let outside specialists make the parts, handle deliveries, or do the accounting." Using the modular model, companies can focus on what they do best, and access the world's best suppliers.

TWO CASES IN POINT

Apparel companies are modular pioneers. Nike and Reebok have prospered by concentrating on their strengths: designing and marketing high-tech, fashionable footwear for sports and fitness. Nike owns one small factory that makes some sneaker parts. Reebok owns no plants. The two rivals contract virtually all footwear production to suppliers in Taiwan, South Korea and other Asian countries.

The electronics industry is evolving into a web of modular companies. Leading the revolution in PCs are such newcomers as Dell, Gateway and Compu-Add. Those companies either buy their products ready-made or purchase all the parts from suppliers, then assemble the machines.

Surprisingly, many suppliers are just as modular as the companies they sell to. Suppliers frequently specialize in design. Cirrus Logic of Fremont, California, is mainly a think tank of 300 engineers who develop sophisticated semiconductors that tie printers and other peripherals to a central computer. Cirrus works closely with Japanese suppliers who manufacture the chips to its specifications.

The Virtual Corporation

Building on the fact that many global businesses already rely on joint ventures and strategic alliances, the newest organizational structure to be proposed for the future is one that is the epitome of partnerships. This fluid and flexible "virtual corporation" would consist of a group of collaborators that could quickly band together to meet a specific market opportunity. Once the opportunity was met, the venture could disband.

In its purest form each independent company that linked with another would contribute only what it regarded as its "core competency." Because each partner would bring its key capability to the partnership—every function and process world-class—it might be possible to create a "best-of-everything" organization.

In a virtual corporation, companies could share costs, skills and access to global markets. Information networks would link up wide-ranging companies and entrepreneurs. Everyone involved would share a sense of "co-destiny" in that the fate of each partner would depend on the others.

A CASE IN POINT

Partnerships, the key attribute of the virtual corporation, are already assuming greater importance in global organizations. Corning Inc. may be the most successful U.S. company for putting together alliances. Its 19 partnerships, which account for nearly 13 percent of earnings last year, have let the company develop and sell new products faster, providing size and power without the bulk.

Says James R. Houghton, chairman of Corning Inc.: "Technologies are changing so fast that nobody can do it all alone anymore. More companies are waking up to the fact that alliances are critical to the future."

A QUESTION OF STANDARDS

At some point in an organization's international development, it must decide which company standards are to be universally accepted and which standards can be left to interpretation within regional values. This task is not as simple as it may at first seem to be. For instance:

○ What does an organization do when its U.S. nonsmoking policy conflicts with the culturally accepted practice of on-the-job smoking within other countries? (Does the organization impose American standards or allow local standards to rule?)

○ How can a company uphold its mandatory drug testing in geographic areas where it is all but impossible to implement? (Does it insist on compliance or look for regional solutions to insure "fitness for duty"?)

○ How does an organization create policies around the major issues of environmental standards, plant safety regulations and business ethics? (Are these to be universal values driven from the United States or regionally determined?)

Exactly how an American organization decides which standards will be global and which should remain regional differs from industry to industry and from company to company. If your organization is grappling with these serious and important issues, you are not alone. Virtually every major international company I talked with told me about their efforts to balance regional and international standards.

Marriott Corporation has decided that there are certain aspects of the business in which there can be no trade-offs. According to Roger Conner, vice president of communications for Marriott Hotels, Resorts and Suites: "There are standards and values that we definitely uphold globally. Our basic philosophy of business stands internationally. We believe that if the organization takes care of its employees, the employees will take care of the customers, and the profits will take care of themselves. We also spend a great deal of time standardizing our operational training. Before our hotel in Warsaw opened in 1990, we had 30 Poles living and working in the Boston Marriott for nine months.

"However, we know that you cannot simply overlay United States standards on Europe, the Pacific Rim or South America. For instance, in the U.S. we offer a service designed to expedite check-in for our business travelers so that they can check directly into their hotel rooms without stopping at the front desk. While it's very popular here, in our European hotels—where people are busy, but time is not of the essence—this same practice would be offensive. European business travelers have definite expectations of good service, and one of those expectations is to be handled a certain way at the front desk."

A GLOBAL CORPORATE CULTURE

In a fast-paced global economy, continuous change becomes the new corporate environment. Companies that cannot adapt to change will not survive. Only corporate cultures that can adapt swiftly to the newest consumer trend, market need or technological breakthrough will stay competitive internationally.

A corporate culture is comprised of values, norms of behavior, systems, policies and procedures that determine how people in the organization act. Much more than any formal statement of rules or structure, it determines who says what to whom, about what, and what kinds of actions then ensue. To adapt to the complexity of the global arena, the culture must allow quick decision making in order to respond to new developments anywhere in the world. It must also provide a common vision and value system to provide guidance for global integration of decentralized management.

ATTRIBUTES OF A GLOBAL CORPORATE CULTURE

Although nothing is universal, the following is a list of attributes which most global organizations are cultivating:

A compelling mission with a global component. A mission offers employees a blueprint of the future—a widely shared image of a realistic, credible and global future for the organization. Weyerhaeuser Company's mission is to be "the best forest products company in the world."

The mission statement tells how an individual or organization makes the world a better place. Apple Computer's unique mission, "To change the world by empowering individuals through personal computing technology," became the driving force of the organization.

A vision of how the organization will fulfill the mission. In a global organization this shared vision serves as a common sense of agenda and helps employees think systematically about how to approach the future.

The vision should address questions like "How will this organization operate globally? How will it create an international presence?" The vision should also inspire and motivate employees to commit to a compelling path for accomplishment of purpose.

A set of core values that align with employee values and tap the energies of workers. Values are the beliefs, principles or purpose the organization stands for, advocates and works to uphold. Values provide clear, inspiring decision-making criteria.

Levi Strauss employees ask, "Is this decision aspirational?" as a way of evaluating choices according to company values. In the Levi Strauss Aspiration Statement, employees are told: "We want our people to feel respected, treated fairly, listened to and involved. Above all, we want satisfaction from accomplishments and friendships, balanced personal and professional lives, and to have fun in our endeavors.

"When we describe the kind of Levi Strauss & Co. we want in the future, what we are talking about is building on the foundation we have inherited: affirming the best of our company's traditions, closing gaps that may exist between principles and practices, and updating some of our values to reflect contemporary circumstances."

Full and open communication practices. Candid communication means that employees understand what "we" as a company are trying to accomplish. It means that everyone is told everything about the company's regional, national and international business strategies and direction.

Wal-Mart's founder, Sam Walton, was one executive who believed in sharing everything possible with employees (or "associates" as they're called at his company). According to Mr. Walton, "The more people know, the more they'll understand. The more they understand, the more they'll care. Once they care, there's no stopping them."

A global perspective. Taking a global view requires all parts of an organization to function in unison, under one plan in which the focus is on doing business on a global scale.

Johnson Wax is a multinational corporation with subsidiaries in 40 countries and licensed manufacturing distributors in seven others. They have 11,000 employees worldwide, with two of every three working overseas. Their transnational perspective is made apparent to employees in many ways:

- ○ "Johnson Wax International" is an internal company newsletter that communicates marketing news of the company on a worldwide basis and provides a medium for making employees fully aware of their multinational character.

- ○ Corporate films have been translated into foreign languages such as French, Dutch, German, Spanish, Italian and Japanese.

- ○ For purposes of communicating corporate philosophy, Johnson Wax instituted the International Editors Program, in which major international subsidiaries select one or more key editors, journalists or reporters to visit the United States for one week and be exposed to Johnson Wax management at the head office in Racine, Wisconsin.

Programs and policies that help employees balance work with personal and family life needs. Helping employees balance their work and personal lives is critical to economic and competitive growth and the ability to retain a productive and motivated work force. According to a 1990 World Leadership Survey conducted by the *Harvard Business Revue*, corporate attitudes toward work and family are fraught with cultural overlays and colored by deeply held personal values. Yet there was global agreement on three win-win practices that benefited both families and organizations:

- ○ Child care at the work site. This practice was overwhelmingly supported by global survey respondents. Companies want productivity; families want time. Child care facilities make it easier for people to work knowing their children are being well looked after.

- ○ Support for dual-career families. Companies around the world are showing strong support for both husbands and wives holding important, paid jobs.

- ○ Flexible work hours. Support for flextime may be in addition to, or an alternative to, child care centers. With this option, family members can provide care for one another.

Ongoing training for employee skills development and education. Global companies can't promise lifetime employment, but by constant training and education they may be able to guarantee their employees lifetime "employability."

Education also plays an increasingly crucial role in our national ability to stay competitive in a global economy. Experts agree that we've got to invest totally in our people. Companies have to get involved with the school systems—with dollars and volunteers. Inside companies we have to upgrade workers' skills through intense and continuous training.

A leading Vancouver, B.C., employer has a unique approach to training its workers: It helps them get educated and then it tells them to leave. While most companies try to keep workers they've trained, Canadian Tire would rather see them go. "Operation Ignition" is both widely loved by employees and provides a productivity payoff for the company. As partner Don Graham explains, "Ninety-five percent of the person-hours put in with our company are tasks that would be best described as entry level. In three months you're going to be as good as you're going to get. Then we have to worry about boredom."

To fight the boredom, Canadian Tire realized there were two choices: Hire dull people who wanted nothing better, or hire bright, energetic people and encourage them to improve themselves. Under the program, bright people are hired and contracted to work no more than 6,000 hours (three years, full-time). After that, they have to leave or go into a management training program. In addition the company pays $3000 toward any course of study the employee chooses.

The payoff for the company is that employees work better while they're at Canadian Tire, productivity rises and wage levels remain low.

A corporate culture in which competition and cooperation are both part of the overall global strategy. Competing successfully in a global environment requires the commitment and cooperation of all of a company's members.

Since this country was founded, it has been an article of faith that competition is essential to the functioning of a free market economy. When we were in school, we competed with our peers for grades and recognition. On the job we were faced with an annual competitive evaluation on which our continued livelihood depended.

Now it is beginning to dawn on us that cooperation, as well as competition, is the secret in the global marketplace. It may seem paradoxical, but increased global competition requires more cooperation. When the competitive scene was less violent, we could afford the luxury of adversarial relations: unions versus management, company versus supplier, company versus dealer, function warfare within the firm, and even company versus customers. Now, competitive and adversarial relationships are no longer affordable. Companies sorely need to create networks of cooperative relationships with customers, suppliers, vendors, employees and even competitors.

It was reported recently that SCA of Sweden and Weyerhaeuser of the United States, two of the world's biggest packaging firms, plan to cooperate in product development and production technology, to the requirements of customers that operate globally. The two companies will exchange commercial and technical information and study the possibility for joint research and development projects with the aim of cutting costs and developing markets through the pooling of their expertise. SCA Packaging is the biggest supplier of corrugated board and container board in Europe, while Weyerhaeuser is number three in the United States.

A work force that cares. At a management forum in Cleveland in March 1987, Joseph Gorman, president and chief operating officer of TRW, described the kind of efforts he thought were needed to bring America back into global competitiveness: "We must have a work force that cares more, knows more and does more. In other words, a work force that is more involved with the success or failure of the enterprise; a work force that cares about and takes pride in the product shipped to the customer."

Tapping the commitment and caring of employees requires mutual trust between management and employees. Employees must believe that management has a workable strategy for the future and will keep workers informed and prepared to meet upcoming challenges. Management needs to trust people—to operate on the premise that people want to achieve, want the organization to succeed, and if given enough of the right information and the authority to do so, will make decisions that benefit themselves and the organization.

An obsession with quality. I don't define quality. You don't define quality. The customer defines quality, and the customer's definition is the only thing that matters. World-class competitors learn this lesson early on. For U.S. business to compete with foreign corporations head-to-head, American business has had to come to grips with the tough realities of multinational definitions of quality.

When Armstrong International Corporation first started selling steam traps in Japan, they received complaints about how the traps looked. Since the Japanese expected no scratches, blemishes or color distortions on their products (although appearance does not affect performance), Armstrong changed to a paint that had more pigment and produced a richer-looking paint job and packed the traps individually so they didn't bump up against one another in shipping.

Questionnaire: How Global Is Your Organization?

1. Does your organizational mission have a global dimension?

2. Does your company source any capital, technology, finance or raw materials from abroad?

3. What percentage of your corporate profits come from overseas?

4. Does your organization utilize innovations in technology and management systems from all over the world?

5. Does your organization recruit, train and repatriate people for overseas assignments?

6. Do your executives and senior managers have international experience?

7. Does your organization offer multicultural sensitivity training programs?

8. Is your company organized into multicultural (or global) work teams?

9. Does your organization provide you with information on its international activities?

10. Does your organization offer courses in doing business in other countries?

CHAPTER

3

Global
Management Skills

*66Future Chief Executive Officers must have an understanding of
how to manage in an international environment . . . to be trained as an
American manager is to be trained for a world that is no longer there.99*

—Lester Thurow, Dean
MIT's Sloan School of Management

*66There is no escaping the fact that a product or service can
be no better, no more sensitive, aesthetic or intelligent than are the
relationships and communication of those who create the product.99*

—Charles Hampton Turner, Professor
London Business School

MANAGEMENT RESPONSIBILITIES

When Levi Strauss stated their aspirations, they outlined the role of management: "What type of leadership is necessary to make our aspirations a reality? New behaviors. Leadership that exemplifies directness, openness to influence, commitment to the success of others, willingness to acknowledge our own contribution to problems, personal accountability, teamwork and trust. Not only must we model these behaviors but we must coach others to adopt them."

At the center of any globalization effort are managers whose role it is to help employees adjust to the complexity, adaptability, uncertainty, diversity and learning that global organizations face in competing on a worldwide basis. A "global manager" is cosmopolitan, effective as an intercultural communicator and negotiator, and leads cultural change on project teams. This type of person can be found in any size organization and in any profession. When operating out of his or her country of origin, the global manager takes actions that ensure that all cultures are afforded equal opportunity in the workplace; that foreign colleagues are made to feel welcome; and that organizational culture responds to the needs and values of the work force, thereby enhancing productivity and performance. When relocated outside his or her own country, the global manager adapts personally to the region and helps others adjust to change. When abroad in a host culture, the manager with a global perspective stays attuned to the difference in cultures while advancing the corporate and common good.

The following directives contain the essence for managerial success and excellence in human, and most especially, international management affairs. Global managers are *most successful* when they:

1. Become incredibly flexible.

Working in a global organization requires that we all learn to live with few fixed rules, and constantly readjust to new organizational goals, objectives and strategies. Through explanation and example managers help workers understand that the most employable people in the future will be those flexible folks who can roll with changes, move easily from one function to another, and operate comfortably in a variety of environments.

2. Support and facilitate a "global mindset."

Global managers motivate people to shift their world view to become inclusive of international trends, markets and innovations. They promote the global vision of the organization and encourage people to think proactively about the opportunities and challenges in an international arena.

While coping with the interdependence of business activity around the world, the cosmopolitan manager also appreciates the effect of cultural differences on standard business practices and procedures.

3. Develop excellent communication skills.

Effective communication skills are crucial to the success of a global manager. Interpersonal communication sets the tone for individual and work team motivation and for job satisfaction in general.

In a foreign country the cosmopolitan manager understands the impact of cultural factors on communication, and is willing to revise and expand behaviors to improve on cross-cultural communication skills.

4. Value and utilize diversity.

Diversity in experience and diversity in perspectives can give an organization the competitive edge. Managers who value a diverse work force (both domestically and internationally) for its richness of ideas and business approaches can best stimulate and utilize the varied perspectives and abilities of all employees.

Global managers operate comfortably in a multinational or pluralistic environment. They are open and flexible in approaching others who represent different cultures and backgrounds, and helpful in finding common ground within these differences.

5. Build local and global work teams.

Whether you call it "high involvement," "employee participation" or "team empowerment," global companies are looking at various ways to move power, knowledge, information and rewards downward through the organization. This requires new management skills and resources.

In addition in global organizations, worldwide teams are being utilized to coordinate and leverage the flow of information and expertise. Senior human resource executives in prominent multinational firms say that building global teamwork is being given top priority to help their companies respond promptly and effectively to competitive challenges and opportunities. Consider this response from the human resource director in one multinational company to an inquiry from the Conference Board: "We have over 75,000 employees and $8 billion in sales, 40 percent of which are from the international arena. Almost all goods sold overseas are produced overseas. We are extremely broad based in terms of products. We sell 55,000 different products. We are in niches. We have small unit sales in many areas that are related in terms of process technology. This makes global teamwork essential."

6. Balance intuitive, right-brained abilities with analytical left-brained skills.

In this chaotic world, stability, predictability and regularity become subordinate to more free-flowing, flexible and malleable thinking systems. In an unpredictable environment all problems cannot be solved, nor all challenges met by right-brained, rational approaches. Managers who can combine analysis with creative and imaginative thinking are ahead of the game.

7. Go beyond management to leadership.

In *Workplace 2000* authors Joseph Boyett and Henry Conn make a case for leadership in the global organization: "In the 1980s, most American workers were managed. Few were led. Americans didn't work for leaders. They worked (or more precisely, 'put in their hours') for managers. As a result, American businesses were overmanaged and underled. Such will not be the case in the future. Workplace 2000 will require leadership, not management. Stable organizations can be managed. Chaotic (global) organizations must be led."

FLEXIBILITY—THE #1 PREREQUISITE FOR GLOBAL MANAGEMENT

Steven Kerr, a management professor at the University of Southern California, says: "The prevailing wisdom we always taught was that an organization had a physical, tangible quality. Companies kept reorganizing to find the right fit. The new view is the organization as kaleidoscope—always changing, always trying to adapt to a continuously changing world."

We all operate in a much more complex environment with far less certainty than ever before. Any manager worth his or her low-sodium salt substitute must learn to create business swiftly in response to fast and fickle markets and economies. He or she must embrace an uncertain future and learn to expose the advantages that come from working with perpetual chaos.

J. Paul Getty once said, "In times of rapid change, our past experience is often our worst enemy." Certainly today, relying solely on skills and abilities honed by past success may inhibit us from embracing the continuous adjustment and learning that must take place.

A CASE IN POINT

In Japan managers are told that life should be a continual process of self-enlightenment. Study and learning should never stop. In Japanese organizations, in fact, the seniors spend more time on thinking and study than their juniors—reading books and articles, meeting with experts, going on study tours to find out how their international competitors work.

Our organizations are in a state of flux, or "permanent white water," for which a whole new set of personal skills and attitudes is necessary. For the global manager the paramount attribute is flexibility.

The managers who are the most flexible have somehow adjusted to a life that appears to be somewhat out of control. They tolerate ambiguity. They stay alert to shifts in their environment. They see uncertainty as an opportunity and have learned ways to take advantage of it. They treat change as an adventure that tests skills and brings forth dormant talents.

If you feel that you would like to be more flexible in your approach to business and management, here is a short list of ways to increase flexibility:

- ○ Take an alternative route to work.
- ○ Start a conversation with a stranger.
- ○ Read a book on a topic you've never investigated.
- ○ Ask to be cross-trained for new skills.
- ○ Have lunch with someone in a different department or company.
- ○ Become part of a cross-functional team.
- ○ Schedule your day and then purposefully alter the schedule.
- ○ Learn a foreign language.
- ○ Take an improvisational acting class.
- ○ Go for a walk with no purpose or destination.
- ○ Play a sport.
- ○ Engage in an activity that friends say is unlike you.
- ○ Raise children.

○ Break a habit.

○ Work in a different industry.

○ Create a gourmet meal without following a recipe.

○ Change your mind.

DEVELOPING A GLOBAL MINDSET

Today, corporations are having to learn to adjust to rapidly changing external conditions and highly competitive situations. Many organizations believe the key to success in this environment is to cultivate a global perspective in their employees.

A mindset is a mental paradigm, a way of filtering how we look at the world. It represents a way of thinking, of being, of orienting to the environment. A global mindset encourages people to expand their view of business to include people, ideas, products and market needs transnationally. It includes everything from constantly looking for unexpected international trends and opportunities, to improving individual cross-cultural teambuilding skills, to attending international business conferences. Fostering a global mindset starts with understanding trends and events in various parts of the world and having a clear idea of their impact (or potential impact) on your organization.

A
CASE
IN
POINT

At McDonald's Corporation building a global mindset begins at Hamburger University, the training center that teaches universal standards and operations to thousands of store managers annually. You don't have to explain the importance of McDonald's international operations to the managers from 65 countries who attend this intensive two-week course. Everyone can see how important global operations are when, at any given time, the university system may utilize the capabilities of translators in 25 languages to communicate with this multinational "student body."

Today, the newest consumer trend or market need can emerge in India or Italy, and the latest technology might be located in Japan or Germany. With a global mindset people scan the world with an expanded perspective and help their companies gain competitive advantage by noticing international trends and needs, innovating to meet those needs, and diffusing the innovation to other global markets.

With a global mindset managers utilize employees from a worldwide labor pool, train people to deal with international business realities, and constantly look for "best practices" from a global arena.

To stay competitive, global companies are making decisions that are good for the entire business worldwide, not just for the United States or any other single country. Employees need to understand the necessity and reality of those choices.

Without a change in people's mindsets, your organization's best vision or global strategy will never fully succeed. Changing to a global corporate culture depends on changing individual attitudes and skills of all employees—executives, managers and hourly workers.

COMMUNICATING A GLOBAL MINDSET

One way to communicate a global mindset is through the company newsletter and other publications. Some multinational companies go the next step and have their newsletters translated from English into another or several other languages before distribution.

A CASE IN POINT

Bancorp Hawaii is a Hawaii-based financial organization with a broad presence throughout the Pacific. From their branches in Hawaii to their international operations, Bancorp's more than 100 offices stretch from as far west as Singapore to as far East as New York. To create a sense of "international family," corporate communications publishes *Spectrum,* a bimonthly employee magazine that features stories and news items from operations globally.

Advances in technology have made it possible for many multinationals to keep in touch with their worldwide operations electronically. From computer faxes to

E-mail to video to satellite conferences, new technologies are helping organizations get the word spread within the company in the fastest manner possible. Still, corporate communication managers tell me that their greatest internal communication challenge is to communicate on a "timely basis"—at least fast enough to stay ahead of the global media.

A CASE IN POINT

Considering the time differences, scheduling global communications can be challenging. ARCO Chemical decided that the best time for its satellite "meetings" between Asia and the United States headquarters is at 7:00 P.M. in Hong Kong (when it is 7:00 A.M. on the East Coast). That way the Asians could stay a little later at work and the Americans could begin a little earlier than usual.

Of course, when it comes to communication, nothing beats face-to-face interaction. Regional and worldwide meetings between international counterparts helps build synergy and global understanding. These interactions, which may take place as often as quarterly, are expensive, time consuming and totally worthwhile.

To maintain a sense of global connectedness, many corporate executives are taking their show on the road and visiting company facilities around the world. There they meet with management and employees to reinforce the ways in which local operations tie into other operations and further support global goals. The challenge there is to make sure that foreign operations understand how they fit into the overall business strategy.

Developing and communicating a global mindset necessitates the constant search for ways to expose your organization to international thinking. Here are a few management strategies for making sure that your organization is thinking globally:

○ Communicate your global mission statement and strategies so that people can understand and believe in them.

○ Communicate your international standing and revenues.

○ Bring in speakers from other global organizations.

○ Bring in speakers from corporate divisions in other countries.

○ Attend at least one international conference each year and share new information with your team members.

○ Review organizational policies on recruiting, training and relocating employees to make sure there is a global emphasis.

○ Find out who the global thinkers are in your organization. Ask employees to send you specific stories about behavior that typifies a global outlook—or use a special project team to collect them.

○ Develop multicultural teams.

○ Look for ways to widely publicize international events and trends.

○ Report on business and technological innovations from all over the world.

○ Post clippings of foreign inventions, technology and management systems that are successful.

○ Celebrate or acknowledge international and ethnic holidays.

○ Encourage employees to learn a foreign language.

○ Encourage employees to travel internationally and to report on their experiences and impressions.

○ Offer courses on how to do business in other countries. Invite all employees to attend.

○ Use your company newsletter to publicize international treaties and laws that may affect your business.

○ Hire managers from other countries.

○ Send U.S. managers to other countries to manage projects.

Peter Harris is the president of ARCO Chemical Asia Pacific. I told him that I thought most managers tended to think regionally, not globally, and asked him if ARCO found it difficult to create a "global mindset." He smiled and said that it was easy to get people to think globally. "I'll tell you what we do at ARCO. Our regional presidents are compensated on the company's global performance. So, although we are all over the world, we think as one business within one major market."

IDEAS FROM EVERYWHERE

Organizations that foster a global mindset know that good ideas can occur anywhere around the world. With this in mind many companies now engage in global "benchmarking." Global benchmarking is a process that focuses on improving organizational processes by seeking out analogous "best practices" of others, then adapting and emulating appropriate practices to the processes within your own company. In short, it is a process for improving processes. It involves understanding your own practices as well as the outward search for best-in-class processes elsewhere. Benchmarking has grown in popularity since the 1980s when Xerox adapted various Japanese techniques to cut its unit production costs in half and to slash inventory costs by two-thirds. Xerox became one of the first American companies to increase its competitiveness through benchmarking.

Managers of global organizations are encouraging benchmarking in everything from marketing practices to how facilities are handled. The key: hunting down best practices nationally and internationally and then developing a strategy for matching what the best will probably be in the future.

Motorola Inc. sent a delegation to Japan in 1985 and saw calculators and computers being made with defect rates 500 to 1,000 times better than at United States electronics makers.

Xerox set out to improve its order-filling process, and went to L.L. Bean Inc. to learn how Bean shipped products so quickly and reliably. While the products shipped were quite different (Bean sells outdoor paraphernalia), the order-filling processes were similar, and that was the system Xerox wanted to benchmark.

COMMUNICATION SKILLS

Beyond being a crucial element for global management, the success of your communication can even affect your health. Individuals with poor communication skills are linked more often to high blood pressure and heart disease. In both the workplace and personal relationships, chronic misunderstandings create resentment and cynicism—conditions adverse to general health.

Good interpersonal communication comes down to listening attentively and speaking clearly, congruently, honestly, compassionately, and with good timing (knowing when and where to communicate).

LISTENING

It is reported that business managers spend close to 50 percent of the working day listening—an amount about equal to the combined time they spend speaking, writing and reading. Yet, according to a survey of 250 Fortune 500 companies, the majority of managers are not considered by their own employees to be effective listeners. In fact, experts say that most of us retain only 20 percent of what we hear.

The consequences of "indifferent listening" include unresolved problems, overlooked situations, ineffectual decisions, costly errors, unattempted projects, misinterpreted ideas and poor employee morale. In contrast, effective listening can help managers foster a willingness to express ideas, interest in sharing information, increased trust and believability, and a stronger desire to achieve and excel.

How Important Is Listening to Your Success?

To assess the role that listening plays in your job, try the following exercise:

On a sheet of paper, record your job responsibilities, then rate listening as a factor in relation to each of these items. (An easy way to do this is to indicate whether listening is "critically relevant," "usually relevant," or "seldom relevant" to the performance of each of your main tasks.) It doesn't matter whether you're the sender or the receiver of communication, or listening most of the time or part of the time. Just consider if listening takes place, and how important it is to you in performing your job.

Many people who perform this exercise find they spend significantly more than 50 percent of their time listening—and as they rise in management, listening tends to become a higher priority. The reason is that when a job grows in complexity and diversity, managers rely more on other people for information and ideas.

To evaluate your own listening skills, ask yourself (and then ask your employees) how well you:

○ set the physical stage for listening by removing physical barriers. (Do you move around your desk to sit side by side or move to another area where the feeling of "equality" is enhanced?)

○ overcome distractions and interruptions. (Do you arrange for someone to screen calls and interrupt only if the call is urgent? Do you select a time and place where you are less likely to be disturbed?)

○ keep an open mind to ideas and information. (Do you ask people to give you their ideas and provide a forum for them to do so?)

○ probe to clarify understanding. (Do you ask leading questions to make sure that you completely understand what the speaker is trying to tell you?)

○ allow people to finish their thoughts. (Do you encourage others to formulate complete ideas and suggestions before you comment?)

○ look for underlying meaning. (Do you stay aware of body language, vocal tone and inflection, and emotional content to help you fully understand the speaker?)

CANDOR, CLARITY, CREDIBILITY

In every employee survey on communication preference, one preference dominates: no matter how good or sophisticated the communication technology, people prefer to get information (face-to-face) from their boss. The most admired and effective managers are the ones who offer information clearly, openly and often. These managers realize that their personal success, as well as the success of the entire organization, increasingly depends on all members of the work force having the same information—and lots of it.

To my way of thinking, verbal communication breaks down into three key components: clarity, credibility and candor.

Clarity. The clear communicator is aware that the message received is often not the same one that was sent. Managers who communicate clearly make every effort to be simple and straightforward, to "over-communicate" by giving out the same information in a variety of forms, and to check that people heard correctly.

The result of clear communication is a work force that knows exactly what the organization stands for, where the company is headed, and how they fit into the overall success of the whole.

Credibility. Managers who become credible communicators are believed and trusted. Employees believe and trust managers who genuinely have their interests at heart, respect them, and who are careful to back any spoken communication with congruent behaviors.

Candor. Candid communicators know the positive power of "telling it like it is." They treat employees like adults, not shielding them from reality as one might a child. They share good and bad news fully and in a timely fashion. Employees report that when they are given honest information, they respond with increased commitment to the organization.

MANAGING DIVERSITY

The role of a global manager demands that he or she must be an effective manager of diversity—on an international scale as well as a local level. Successful managers of diversity believe that cultural diversity is an asset. They therefore value and encourage the different talents, perspectives, attitudes and ways of solving problems that multiculturalism brings. And they channel this multicultural force into a single unifying direction.

Every organization must deal with diversity in a variety of situations. There may be diverse departmental cultures within the organization, as defined by different functions within the same company—manufacturing and sales may represent quite disparate points of view, for example. Of course, if you have ever joined two organizations by merger or acquisition, you have first hand knowl-edge of the challenges of trying to blend totally unique corporate cultures into one unit.

The changing composition of the American work force has made clear the need to manage ethnic, racial and gender diversity issues whether or not you leave national borders. The white male who traditionally dominated the work force will be reduced to 39 percent by the year 2000. As we move into the next century, the new entries into the U.S. work force will be 85 percent white women, immigrants, blacks, hispanics and Asians. While it is true that Americans hold much in common—many beliefs, values and goals—most of us learned to be members of our own culture first. Race, ethnicity, gender and class values are instilled from infancy on.

Here are a few examples of diversity in the workplace:

> A Latino manager starts a budget-planning meeting by chatting casually and checking with his new staff on whether everyone can get together after work. His boss frets over the delay and feels they are taking an awful lot of time getting down to business. A white American interviewing a black American for a job thinks the man is not listening. The applicant feels the manager is talking down to him. A native American working in a mainstream organization gets an unreasonable request from her manager. She keeps her head down and walks away.

These kinds of scenarios are occurring more frequently as the North American work force becomes more culturally diverse. Many domestic businesses are now almost in the same position as international companies because of the diversity of their employees. In a Digital Equipment plant near Boston, Massachusetts, the 350 employees come from 44 countries and speak 19 different languages. So diverse is the plant that announcements are frequently written in English, Chinese, French, Spanish, Portuguese and Haitian Creole.

Managers are finding that dealing with employees from varying cultures or languages can be tense. Misunderstandings can crop up because of different social styles, behavior toward authority figures, and even speaking patterns.

The misunderstanding in the black-white interview example was likely caused by culturally different speaking patterns. When middle-class white Americans talk, the speaker usually looks away from the listener, turning toward him or her from time to time to make a point. The listener gazes directly at the speaker, then occasionally nods visibly to make it clear the point is understood.

With inner-city blacks, the pattern is almost reversed. The listener looks away from the speaker, turning toward him or her occasionally to indicate understanding. The nods are almost imperceptible.

The white manager sees the interviewee looking away and may interpret this as rudeness, thinking: "He can't meet my gaze." Because he hasn't picked up on the slight nods, the manager may also feel he hasn't made his point. He then begins to "hyper-explain," or talk down. The signal this gives to the interviewee is: "He thinks I'm stupid."

In the case of the Latino manager, his boss may regard the conversation as social chitchat—but the Latino culture teaches that building relationships is often critical to working together. In fact, the Latino may regard the boss as a little insensitive and too eager to "get down to business."

As for the native American, she might just walk away because elders are never questioned in her culture.

Differences in gender can also cause misunderstandings. Males assume that female colleagues grew up in the same culture. It's not so. To grow up female in the United States is completely different from growing up male. Boys' psychology is oriented to think of the world in terms of win-lose. Women are often more adept at handling interpersonal situations. A female may ask, "Do you think we should invite X to this meeting?" when she means, "I think we should invite X." Many women have learned to speak in tentative or questioning tones to avoid appearing too aggressive.

While each cultural style has its strengths and weaknesses, and real differences frequently do exist, additional problems arise when one group tends to stereotype another. Ruth, a female project manager in an engineering firm, has prepared an excellent report. Her male colleagues discount the report because of their stereotypical belief that "women can't handle that kind of highly technical assignment."

To avoid cultural stereotyping, we must stay aware of differences among cultures and of personal idiosyncrasies and preferences. The management goal is to create a balance between cultural sensitivity (with the generalities such understanding promotes) and judging and accepting all people as unique individuals.

Dealing with foreign-born employees working in the United States takes one set of management skills, but managing a work force of nationals on their home soil requires special cultural sensitivities. Managers need to be open and responsive to national differences and local interests in all the host countries where they operate. Each culture has its expectations for the roles of boss and subordinate, and for working relationships. Each culture has its own way of making decisions, learning new skills, responding to authority, and even thinking and reasoning. Different cultures have different work ethics and motivations. On top of all this, every organization operates within the country's culture and within its own special culture—just as our U.S. organizations do—so that effective management styles at a Swiss bank might be different from management practices at a Swiss pharmaceutical company. When it comes to international management, there is no "one style fits all" that will succeed in every case. You must stay aware of the realities in your particular circumstances.

A CASE IN POINT

When a rich vein of ore was found in the Andes, Americans rushed in to develop the mining. But it was hard for them to keep local workers, even though the Americans offered housing, hot meals, movies, hot water and all kinds of perks. The workers seemed to prefer the French, who offered them none of the comforts provided by the U.S. company. After some time, the U.S. company figured out what was happening: the French paid workers by the hour, and the people of the Andes wanted to be able to come and go without question. Only when the Americans switched to an hourly pay basis were they able to attract the workers.

MANAGING TEAMS

Managers have always handled two main jobs: supervising people and gathering, processing and transmitting information. But in growing numbers of companies, self-managed work teams are taking over such standard supervisory duties as scheduling work, maintaining quality, even administering pay and vacations.

Meanwhile, the ever-expanding power and the dwindling cost of computers have transformed the way information can be handled and disseminated.

There are many examples of organizations that have empowered employees through teamwork. Some 60 percent of General Mills plants have already been converted to "high performance work systems." Self-managed teams are informed of marketing plans and production costs, and handle everything from scheduling production to rejecting products not up to quality standards. Team members receive bonuses based on plant performance. The approach has produced significant gains in productivity, and the company is now moving to spread it to all operations.

In some organizations teams are deciding the future of the company. Like many companies today, Air Products and Chemicals, Inc., is reengineering their work systems. To facilitate this process they set up five cross-functional teams of ten persons per team. Each of these Quality Improvement Teams (QIT) was assigned an area of responsibility: either morale and teamwork, mission and resources, employee development, customer service or communications. QITs were trained and sent into the field to discover needed improvements; they met for one year and then reported to headquarters on the issues that needed attention. After reviewing and sorting the lists, they were returned to the teams and sent out once more to gather recommendations for solutions to the problem issues. The 50 recommendations were prioritized and assigned for immediate management attention.

Teams are becoming the very backbone of some companies' global competitive thrust. In the 1980s, foreign competitors—especially Japan—moved into the United States with cheaper basic machine tools. Hundreds of U.S. tool firms went out of business. Cincinnati Milacron, a leader in the production of advanced machine tools, survived by redesigning its entire product line to create a new series of globally competitive machines. The base of their effort is the use of special, multidisciplined employee-involvement teams that define and solve problems. These "Wolfpack" teams of eight to ten employees are drawn from different areas like engineering, marketing, accounting and manufacturing. Milacron now has about twenty Wolfpack teams at work. Each team, headed by a leader called a "killer," is charged with improving the quality of Milacron's machines while removing up to 40 percent of the cost and 40 percent of the components.

Today Cincinnati Milacron is building and installing the largest project in its history, a $58.95 million flexible machining complex for Alenia, Italy's largest aerospace firm. "I don't know of anybody in the world who could put together a bigger automated factory system," said Roy Ross, Milacron's president. "This shows the scope of technology we have developed out of our Wolfpack program. If we did not have the Wolfpack program, we would not have this order today."

To obtain this kind of involvement in the work process, employees are being made "associates" or "partners" to management and given the responsibilities and the rights of partnership. Within this kind of work environment, managers today must increasingly obtain the consent of the people they manage. In many ways this puts managers in a much tougher role because they cannot rely on title or unquestioning loyalty and obedience to get things done.

Global teamwork is being given top priority to help organizations respond promptly and effectively to competitive challenges and opportunities. As the world intertwines in a truly global marketplace and economy, the events in one country can have almost immediate ramifications for businesses in other parts of the world. So, whether their businesses are worldwide in scope or limited to the United States, major American companies are finding global teamwork essential.

Bull Information Systems, with 38,000 employees in over 100 countries, uses Cross-Functional Core Teams that lay the foundation for employees from different countries to come together to solve problems and complete projects. Although Core Teams can work in any area of the business, the first "pilot" Core Teams at Bull were established in 1990 for developing products and product delivery.

While the teams at Bull do not make strategic market or technology decisions, these cross-functional and multicultural teams are accountable from start to finish for a product's success. Core Team members are empowered to plan the integration, coordination, negotiation and communication of all aspects of the project. Their responsibilities might include accelerating design schedules, reevaluating forecasts or even deciding that the best option for the company is to discontinue development of the product.

In the past American organizations used global teams primarily to provide counsel and advice to the decision-making top executive. Today, global teams are being established for a variety of purposes, including overall strategic planning.

Assessing the Multicultural Team

Indrei Ratiu, a founding partner of Paris-based Intercultural Management Associates, has suggested the following criteria for evaluating the effectiveness of a multicultural team, as printed in an *International Consulting News* article:

○ Do members work together with a common purpose (something that is spelled out and felt by all to be worth fighting for)?

○ Has the team developed a common language or procedure (a common way of doing things, a process for holding meetings)?

○ Does the team build on what works (learning to identify the positive actions before being overwhelmed by negatives)?

○ Does the team attempt to spell out things within the limits of the cultural differences involved (limit the mystery level by directness and openness regardless of cultural origins of participants)?

○ Do the members recognize the impact of their own cultural programming on individual and group behavior (deal with, not avoid the differences in order to create a synergy)?

○ Does the team have fun (within successful multicultural groups, the cultural differences become a source of continuing surprise, discovery and amusement rather than irritation or frustration)?

WHOLE-BRAIN THINKING

Charles Handy writes in *The Age of Unreason,* "We are now entering the Age of Unreason, when the future, in so many areas, is there to be shaped by us and for us—a time when the only prediction that will hold true is that no predictions will hold true; a time, therefore, for bold imaginings in the private life as well as public, for thinking the unlikely and doing the unreasonable."

In 1981 Roger Sperry was awarded the Nobel Prize for his proof of the split-brain theory. According to this theory the two hemispheres of the brain have different, but overlapping functions. The right and left hemispheres of the brain each specialize in distinct types of thinking processes.

The left side of the brain not only controls the right side of the body but is also responsible for analytical, linear, verbal and rational thought. It is a left-brain function you rely on when balancing your checkbook, remembering names and dates, or setting goals and objectives.

The right hemisphere controls the left side of the body and is holistic, imaginative, nonverbal and artistic. Whenever you recall someone's face, become engrossed in a symphony, or simply daydream, you are engaging in right-brain function.

Since most concepts of thinking (in this culture) come from Greek logic, left-brained processes are the ones most exercised and rewarded in school. While right-brain processes may be highly valued in many other cultures—some cultures consider intuition or "feelings" about a situation to be extremely important—right-brain thinking is not traditionally rewarded in our education system.

The idea of whole-brain thinking is not meant to discredit the left-brain skills that you have already developed, but simply to understand the advantages of augmenting those skills with the more creative functions of right-brain thinking.

Connecting creative thinking to prevailing management practice is crucial in an era of global competition. Fresh ideas have become a company's most precious raw material. To remain competitive, corporations must engage in "kaizen," a Japanese term meaning continuous improvement. Management must give employees and departments license to use creativity to improve performance. Unfortunately, most companies restrict the use of creativity to the art or public relations department. Yet creativity isn't a mystical force or extraordinary talent only possessed by a lucky few. Discouraging creative thinking prevents managers from making the best use of individual talents, aptitudes and abilities. Problem-solving skills suffer and management loses opportunities for innovation and entrapreneuring.

As a manager, learning to use more of your own creative abilities will allow you to be more confident in confronting situations requiring original ideas and imaginative solutions. Encouraging the creativity of your team or sub-ordinates can provide fresh insights and new perspectives on even routine elements of job performance.

Successful companies are those best able to adapt to rapidly changing markets, values and work force. And that kind of rapid adapting is greatly enhanced by applying the creative process. Creativity enables an organization to view problem solving as a creative opportunity.

At General Electric researchers spend at least an hour a day thinking about technology that might be transferred. They're also required to spread their ideas throughout GE to find new product applications. A technology invented to protect coal-spraying nozzles in an experimental locomotive led to a new generation of energy-saving light bulbs. Sophisticated coating and machining techniques developed for airplane engines were adopted by the company's power-generating division.

One of the strongest roadblocks to creative thinking in organizations is a reluctance to look beyond acceptable or easy models of behavior and thinking. There is an old joke about a drunk who lost his keys one night in a dark alley. He circled around and around the corner street light looking for his keys "because the light is better here." Creativity is looking where the light isn't.

Here are some other barriers that keep us from being as creative as we might be:

○ Getting stuck on one "right" answer

○ Conformity to established patterns and rules

○ Premature or uniformed judgments

○ Fear of failure

○ Fear of looking like a fool

○ Lack of self-confidence in one's own creative abilities

○ Reluctance to entertain other people's "different" ideas

Everyone has creative potential. Creativity is not an ability that you either have or do not have. It is not a talent; it is a way of operating, a mode of behaving. The most creative people simply have acquired a facility for getting themselves into a particular mood which allows their creative abilities to function. Researchers have described this particular facility as an ability to play with ideas—to explore them, not for any immediate practical purpose, but just for the enjoyment of playing, the delight of exploration.

Developing the habit of creativity can be a gift to yourself, your workplace and those you manage. Here are some guides to help you on your journey to richer and more creative ways of doing business:

○ **Accept the fact that you are creative.** Break the barriers of self-doubt, preconceived values and habit that block the creative flow.

○ **Expand your horizons.** Learning in many different fields helps you open your mind to alternatives, to see connections. Ask for (and value) the diversity of opinion around you—your employees, your customers, your coworkers, your family, and people from totally different fields.

○ **Create a climate for creativity.** Give yourself the time and incentive to generate and "play" with a host of ideas before judging any of them. Develop patterns or rituals that you can count on to put you in a creative, playful, "open" mode of thinking and behaving.

○ **Keep a journal.** A journal is not simply a record of events. Use it to keep track of ideas, observations, perceptions and insights. Keep it by your bed to record your dreams.

○ **Follow your hunches.** Pay attention to your intuitions and "gut feelings." An idea will keep nagging you until you figure it out. Stay with persistent thoughts and images. They may lead to a breakthrough.

○ **Develop a positive attitude.** Sounds like a cliché, but positive emotions do foster creative thoughts, while negative emotions tend to block creativity.

○ **Exercise your right brain.** Creative games, imagery, puzzles—all help to shape up your creative faculty and your imagination.

FROM MANAGER TO LEADER

In our postindustrial world it is not the capital assets nor the number of employees that will determine a company's fate, but rather the intensity of motivation and innovation from its work force.

People want to work. A recent Gallop poll found that 70 percent of respondents would continue to work even if they had enough money to retire. However, fewer than 40 percent would continue in their current jobs. Over 60 percent of the work force want out from under their present bosses. These people are tired of being over-managed and under-led. They want their managers to also be leaders.

Certainly, being a leader in today's global organization is not easy. In *On Leadership* John Gardner states the leadership skills needed for global competitiveness this way: "Leaders must have some grasp of economic realities and some comprehension of the basic framework within which scientific and technological change takes place. They must gain an understanding of the political process. They must comprehend the pitfalls of power and the sources of human conflict. Corporate executives must understand the relationship between government and the private sector and must comprehend the national and world economy. In this interdependent world, leaders should come to know some culture other than their own, and all high-level leaders must understand international issues in depth."

Leaders get things done in organizations by inspiring and motivating others toward a common purpose. They get people to work together by concentrating on what everyone has to offer and how everyone can gain. While the manager's authority is legitimized by his or her position, the leader's authority is legitimized by his or her vision and ability to communicate that vision to followers. In his book *Leadership Is an Art,* Max DuPree says, "Leadership is more tribal than scientific, more a weaving of relationships than amassing information."

Today our organizations need the creativity, innovation, participation and commitment of all their employees. Compliance—just following orders—is not enough. We need fully participating employees who feel they have an emotional stake in the business. In this reality the global manager must be a new kind of leader: one who builds collaboration, teamwork and partnerships, and fosters collective innovation.

Here are some differences to be aware of as you find yourself moving from manager to leader:

From Manager:	To Leader:
Uses power to persuade others and to "sell" ideas	Uses power in the service of others
Knows the right answer	Seeks many inputs for answers
"Hands-on" involvement	Empowers people
Gains compliance	Builds commitment
Enforces rules	Gives people clear choices
Keeps a strict routine	Breaks free of routine; gets rid of useless habits
Punishes failure	Analyzes failure
Takes success for granted	Analyzes and celebrates success
Protects people by withholding unpleasant truths	Communicates candidly
Motivates through "pep" talks	Motivates through challenge and variety in work
Keeps teamwork in the office	Encourages social gathering and team "play"
Builds dependence	Creates new leaders from followers
Sets all goals	Negotiates goals with work group
Rewards individuals	Shows how greatest gains can come from collaboration
Management planning driven by technique	Management planning driven by vision and values

Sublimates individual for the good of the organization	Understands the mutual dependence of the individual and the organization and looks for common benefit
Focuses on operating in their area of assigned responsibility	Focuses beyond assigned area to meeting needs of the entire organization or of society as a whole
Tries to do things right	Tries to do the right things
Controls and commands	Motivates and inspires
Follows strict chain of command	Deals with anyone necessary to get the job done

USC business professor Burt Nanus identifies global business leaders as those people within an organization who can "take charge, make things happen, dream the dreams and translate them into reality, attract the voluntary commitment of followers and energize them, and transform organizations into new entities with greater potential for survival and growth and excellence."

CHAPTER

4

Managing Change

❝The continuing reorganization of work itself is part of a social transformation as massive and wrenching as the industrial revolution.❞

—John Sculley, Former President
Apple Computer

❝One of the big lessons I've learned is that change has no constituency. People like the status quo. They like the way it was. When you start changing things, the good old days look better and better.❞

—Jack Welch, CEO
General Electric

THRIVING ON CHANGE

Reengineering, restructuring, downsizing, right-sizing, mergers, acquisitions, new technologies, new markets, new customer demands, government regulations, global competition and a vacillating world economy all add up to one thing—CHANGE—and plenty of it!

Business Week magazine entitled its 1992 year-end issue "Reinventing America." In it they spoke of a "flexible tomorrow," in which: "The successful company of the future will be an adaptive one, in which change replaces stability as a key trait. What's right today isn't likely to be right tomorrow or the next day. There is an awareness that the reinvention of the corporation is going to go on forever."

This is a relatively new perception. Not long ago, management thought that change was an event. Now we know that it is a process—a continual process. As author and management consultant Tom Peters put it: "Managers must take chaos as a given and learn to thrive on it."

It is now clear that global change will be a way of life in the 1990s and beyond. Volatile political, economic, competitive and customer patterns will demand continuous change—until this constant reorganization becomes part of the business itself.

To compete internationally during these turbulent times, organizations must continually operate in a state of transformation. Those organizations which advance change most effectively gain competitive advantage.

In his recent book, *A Manager's Guide to Globalization,* Stephen Rhinesmith states: "Today's manager in a global organization is responsible for more than just business strategies and tactics to achieve organizational objectives. He or she must think systematically and open-endedly regarding organizations as cultures that must adapt and change to survive. The people inside the organization must be managed in a way that enables and allows them to work freely with change."

In the past change management was thought to be required on a situational basis only. The traditional model for managing change was to employ skills that first prepared people for the change (unfreeze people from current behaviors), then guided them through the change (mold new behaviors), and finally, helped them integrate the completed change (freeze new behaviors). Within this tidy strategy there was at least a semblance of control and predictability. Managers today know that in an era of overlapping, concurrent and accelerating change, this management model is no longer valid. We have moved from *the* change (an event) to change as continuous process. That takes an entirely new perspective and approach.

Change managers today wrestle with the challenge of evoking commitment to the organization's mission and objectives while continually responding to an environment that is ambiguous, unreliable and unpredictable. On top of that, one basic dilemma management faces is that change must be freely adopted by the people it affects, most of whom resist its intrusion. To further complicate the job, some degree of organizational structure and formality must coexist with the instability and free flow of an unknowable future. So not only must managers take Tom Peters' advice and learn to thrive on chaos, they must help others in the organization learn to do the same.

EMBRACING CHAOS

Chaos is a term from physics to describe a border area between stability and utter confusion. Global managers must help their employees to seek out chaos rather than defend against it, expect uncertainty rather than demand predictability, and look for the unique opportunities inherent in continuous change.

This is no easy task. Everyone faces an unknowable future with some trepidation. You really have no idea what the long-term future holds for you, your employees or the organization. And it's easy to understand the reluctance of many people to embrace fundamental structural shifts that do not always benefit them personally.

We all agree that the workplace is in transition—and will continue to be for some time—but the positive ramifications of living in transitional times are that you get to be a partner in the creation of what is to follow. Some researchers hold a hopeful picture of the workplace to come. In January of 1993 *Fortune* magazine predicted: "The workplace will be healthier, saner, more creative, and yet more chaotic—like nature itself."

NEW MANAGEMENT DEFINITION AND SKILLS

There are enormous changes going on in the diffusion of power in a competitive organization. Companies that want to react quickly to changes in the marketplace have to put more and more accountability, authority and information into the hands of the people who are closest to the customer. If the people on the front line are really the key to our success, then the manager's job is to help those people and the people they serve. That goes against the traditional assumption that the manager is expected to know everything that is going on and to be in control of subordinates' activities. Max DuPree, the chief executive officer of Herman Miller, sees the potential difficulty ahead for management: "The primary issue of the 1990s will be to help managers understand it is not their job to supervise or motivate, but to liberate and enable."

Managers need the consent, cooperation and commitment of employees, and consent cannot be forced from people. It must be freely given. So management practices are moving from coercion and manipulation ("the carrot and the stick") to cooperation. And as a result, an entirely new definition of management is emerging. The classic definition of management used to be "working with and through people for organizational objectives." Now management is being redefined as "creating an environment in which people get the job done," or even "the act of relationship building in order to achieve mutual objectives for mutual gain." To operate effectively within these new definitions, today's management concepts include networking, nurturing, open communication, translating new roles and responsibilities to employees, trust building, letting people learn from their own trials and errors, and looking at how best to get things done so that everyone benefits ("mutuality").

This concept of mutuality is a new but increasingly universal discovery of successful organizations. The University of Western Ontario found that "We must acknowledge and deal with the fact that inviting uncertainty, the risk of occasional failure and a certain amount of dislocation demand that we respect the loyalty to self that a staff member must have. The institution cannot expect an individual to make great sacrifices to the university at personal expense. We will not succeed if we fail to foster an environment in which approaches to the achievement of personal and institutional goals are mutually reinforcing."

CHANGING RULES OF RELATIONSHIP

There is no doubt that we are entering a corporate economic reality that is increasingly more bare-knuckled and tough-minded. Employees in all companies bemoan the fact that the old relationship between the employer and employee is gone. Companies no longer offer job security, and employees are being asked to assume full responsibility for their careers, retirement and job satisfaction.

The rules of relationship have indeed changed, but they have not been changed arbitrarily by the companies. They have been changed by the new global work environment which forces companies to work harder and be more accountable for themselves. Every organization has to learn how to do more with less, and in a continually changing environment, no company in any industry can guarantee real security.

To keep a spirit of commitment in this changing work environment, mangers help employees understand *why* and *how* the rules of relationship between the company and its work force have been fundamentally altered. They help people prepare realistically for future personal and organizational challenges.

In a corporate world that softens every blow with positive rhetoric about employees being members of the family, there are bound to be problems. Tough decisions in the corporate interest appear contrary to all mutual expectations. The result of a firing or restructuring, for example, can be hostility and an affront to the dignity of both sides.

Companies that communicate fully and candidly about today's business environment allow people to prepare realistically and make informed decisions. We are entering a future that will encourage corporate disruption. Lifetime employment is dead. Short-term and contract-based employment represents the wave of tomorrow. Traditional concepts of loyalty will not survive. Cosmetic cover-ups with managerial double-talk only makes things worse. People need to know what they can expect from their employers—as well as what is expected of them. Managers who communicate honestly and openly with their employees—helping them understand the kinds of choices and oppor-tunities available—are the managers who really assist people in adapting to new realities.

As time goes by, workers and companies will be more accustomed to negotiating voluntary relationships that benefit both parties. Business will benefit from an abler, more flexible, and vastly more responsible work force, job holders will get more respect, and their work may become more engaging as employers seek employees' creative input.

Regardless of the industry you represent, chances are your organizational relationship is already changing in at least some of the following dimensions:

Old Relationship:	New Relationship:
Paternalistic	Professional
Dependent	Responsible
Blind loyalty	Mutual respect
Passive	Accountable
Insulated from competitive climate	Driven to beat competition
Time rewarded	Performance rewarded
Follow orders	Exercise initiative
Employment security	"Employability" through constant skills building
Boss-subordinate	Partnership
Change- and risk-averse	Continuous adapting

MANAGING THE FUTURE

Looking ahead, business will be driven more and more by the intensity of global competition and the corresponding need for corporations to manage operating costs. In the United States, schools are obsessed with thinking about the past. We now need to also learn how to think about the future in a systematic way. Even though no one can accurately predict many of the events that will affect us, managers can help people prepare for change (and become more flexible in their thinking) by encouraging them to envision a variety of future "possible" environments. Here are the steps:

O Look for future possibilities—trends, new technology, market needs, social forces—and plot scenarios that could result from these changes.

O List the choices that are available to benefit, influence or respond to future scenarios.

O In light of these various prospects, discuss what is likely to happen if your organization continues in its current direction.

O Propose alternative directions for the organization.

O Discuss the kinds of training and skill building that would be necessary to prepare personally and professionally for possible futures.

Another way to prepare for changes in the future is to note and discuss the latest organizational practices of leading edge companies. Right now, companies as diverse as General Electric, Xerox, General Motors' experimental spinoff, Saturn, Southern Gas Company, Goodyear Tire & Rubber, Johnson & Johnson, Hallmark Cards, Pepsico, Colgate-Palmolive and Texas Instruments are embracing concepts that would have been unthinkable just a few years ago. Even if these are new concepts to you, don't be surprised if in the near future your organization is following some of these corporate trends:

O The bully boss is out; the boss-as-coach is in. In this brave new business world, managers recognize that workers closest to the process understand it best. So the good manager listens and removes hurdles. (Do you have the necessary sensitivity and training for this transition?)

O Business must concentrate obsessively on pleasing customers. The success of companies like discount chain Wal-Mart stores, which focus totally on serving customers, is invoked over and over. (How are your customer service skills?)

O Big is bad and must be broken into manageable parts. While the optimum size depends on the company, William Ouchi, a professor at the John E. Anderson Graduate School of Management at the University of California, says: "Companies should never grow beyond the limits of knowledge of a normal human being. We will see large scale disaggregation of big companies into their constituent pieces." (How might your organization be resized?)

○ Instead of simply downsizing an organization, companies are radically restructuring based on redesigning—or reengineering—how the work gets done. Management consultant Michael Hammer explains it using a metaphor: "If all you do is try to flatten your existing organization, you'll kill it. The fat is not waiting around on top to be cut. It's marbled in, and the only way you get it out is by grinding it out and frying it out." (Are you aware of unnecessary steps taken in your work process?)

○ Once work meant a forty-hour-a-week, full-time job that could last a lifetime. Today more than 30 million Americans are employed as temps, part-timers and independent contractors. Called the contingent work force, this flexible segment of the U.S. labor force accounts for more than one-quarter of civilian jobs, according to one study. (Is your function one that could be contracted out, handled by part-time employees, or taken over by independent contractors? If so, how could you use this foresight to create an opportunity for yourself?)

MANAGING VALUES

People have always asked value-laden questions. The following graffiti were spray-painted onto a university wall: Who are we? Why are we here? How did we get here? Where are we going? How are we going to get there? Should we bring sandwiches?

The role of the global manager is to understand work force values and to position change in ways that enable people to identify with its corresponding values. To do that, employees must believe that the organization is evolving in ways that meet the long-term interests of employees, of the organization and of the community and society.

Global managers must also move beyond values by transforming general statements of values to concrete behaviors and work practices. In any organization there is a gap between what the company says it stands for and what it feels like to work there. It is that gap between what is articulated and the way things really are that erode trust and inhibit action. The more management can narrow the gap, the more people's energies can be released toward constructive purposes.

Many years ago Studs Turkel wrote in his landmark book, *Working*, that the Americans he interviewed were looking for something more at work than just a paycheck: "It is about a search . . . for daily meaning as well as daily bread, for recognition as well as cash, for astonishment rather than stupor; in short, for a sort of life rather than a Monday through Friday sort of dying. Perhaps immortality, too, is part of the quest. To be remembered was the wish, spoken and unspoken, of the heroes and heroines of this book."

The dictionary defines "value" as something regarded as desirable, worthy or right, as a belief, standard or precept. Values are deep-seated, pervasive standards that influence all aspects of our behavior—our personal "bottom line." Personal values are also deeply emotional and often very idealistic.

In organizations values are especially critical during times of abrupt change and persistent uncertainty. They give us operating standards when the policies and habits that normally govern our actions may no longer be appropriate. As noted by Robert Haas, CEO of Levi Strauss: "A company's values—what it stands for, what its people believe in—are crucial to its competitive success."

In their corporate research, Tom Peters and Bob Waterman concluded that successful companies often embraced just a few basic values or beliefs, such as:

○ A belief in being the best

○ A belief in the importance of the details of execution, the "nuts and bolts" of doing the job well

○ A belief in the importance of people as individuals

○ A belief in superior quality and service

○ A belief that most members of the organization should be innovators with a corresponding willingness to support failure

○ A belief in the importance of informality to enhance communication

○ Explicit belief in the importance of economic growth and profits

As you think through the driving values that govern daily life and work in your organization, ask yourself:

○ How do you communicate these key values?

○ How do you reinforce them?

○ How do you personally demonstrate these values?

○ How do your policies, procedures, training and reward structure reflect your values?

THE ORGANIZATION AS AN AGENT OF SOCIAL CHANGE

Some organizations are currently positioning their business as an agent of social change. The Body Shop, headquartered in England, is a remarkable example of financial success and corporate-social responsibility. The founder and chief executive officer of this international cosmetic company is Anita Roddick, who has laid out their five principles:

1. To sell cosmetics with a minimum of hype and packaging

2. To promote health rather than glamour and reality rather than instant regeneration

3. To use naturally based, close-to-source ingredients

4. To do no animal testing

5. To respect the environment

When you get the Body Shop catalogue, you also find out about orphans in Romania, Amnesty International, ways to save the rain forest, and other social causes. Every Body Shop around the world does community action of their choice on company time. When asked about the low employee turnover rate, Ms. Roddick replied, "What moves employees to stay with us is not the moisture cream. It is our high moral code."

THE ORGANIZATION AND THE ENVIRONMENT

Respect for the environment is a value that organizations around the globe are responding to. Ernst Winter and Son is a German manufacturer of diamond tools. Since 1972 environmental protection has been one of its corporate aims, and by the late 1980s there was a complete model for environmental business management. Here are just a few of the environmentally sound practices pioneered by Winter:

○ Conduct an environmental audit and make sure work areas and things like lighting and materials are healthy ones.

○ Buy only from environmentally responsible suppliers.

○ Tie bonuses and promotions to environmental responsibility, and train employees in those areas.

○ Offer counseling in employees' homes for things like reducing water consumption or saving energy.

○ Create an environmental senior position reporting directly to the CEO.

○ Elicit employee suggestions for environmental safeguards.

○ Locate plants only in areas that are not polluted.

○ Utilize state-of-the-art disposal systems as well as manufacturing processes.

○ Give employees time off to volunteer for environmental causes.

THE SPIRITUAL ORGANIZATION

Managing values aligns employees with the organization and forges an emotional connection. Some have likened employees' emotional connection to a corporation as having religious overtones. Peter Senge, professor at MIT Sloan School of Management, states: "A corporation can't save your soul, but it can stand in for the age-old idea of people collectively pursuing a path that has real meaning to them."

Mixing spiritual and commercial aims is awkward, one reason why so few big corporations try it. ServiceMaster Company is an exception to that rule. Headquartered near Chicago, ServiceMaster's international army of 15,000 employees manages housekeeping, food service, clinical equipment maintenance and other services for several markets. ServiceMaster heads the Fortune Service 500 Companies list with an average return on equity for the past decade of a whopping 63.7 percent.

The philosophy of ServiceMaster is expressed by their four objectives:

To honor God in all we do. Our company recognizes God's sovereignty in all areas of our business. Our objective is to apply consistently the principles, standards and values of the Bible in our business attitudes.

To help people develop. Our company believes that people grow with the challenge and opportunity for achievement that requires an individual to stretch. Employees will be encouraged to expand their abilities and potential through the company's educational and training programs and through education available outside of the company. In recruiting, developing and training employees, the company will provide an equal opportunity for all.

To pursue excellence. Our company accepts the responsibility continually to seek better methods to render current and new services to its customers at better value. Our trademarks and service marks stand for excellence. We are committed to continue serving each of our customers with a pursuit of excellence.

To grow profitably. Our company sees growth in revenue while maintaining an adequate profit both as the material means of achieving the other objectives and as a measurement means of the company's values to its customers, employees and shareholders. Our company is committed to use profit with a sense of stewardship and responsibility to employees and customers while providing a means for profitable investing. We are also determined to share these benefits of the free enterprise system domestically and throughout the world.

BUILDING CHARACTER

"The '80s were about style and life-style," says clothing designer and entrepreneur Susie Tompkins of Esprit de Corp, headquartered in San Francisco. "The '90s are about soul-searching . . . about encouraging volunteerism. Before, we gave our employees French lessons, sent them on river trips—all of those personal things. Now, we're giving them character-building opportunities." To support employees' volunteer work, Esprit allows up to ten hours per month of paid leave, to be matched by a similar amount of the employee's own time. Esprit's mission statement was devised by a collective group of employees: "Be informed. Be involved. Make a difference."

Darryl Hartley-Leonard, president of Chicago-based Hyatt Hotels, would agree. Crediting an idea hatched by a regional vice president, Hartley-Leonard has launched the Hyatt F.O.R.C.E. (Family of Responsible and Caring Employees). Every manager receives four paid days off a year to volunteer. In a given month about 1,000 Hyatt employees are out involved in the community.

Values Principles

Principle 1   People tend to think, talk about and do what they value.

Principle 2   People tend to commit emotionally to entities—other people, organizations, political parties, religions, etc.—whose values reflect their own.

Principle 3   People tend to withdraw emotional commitment from entities that compromise their values.

THE VALUES MATCH

Do you know what your employees value? If not, an exercise you might like to try is to ask your work group to write out their values, then to look for their personal connections to similar values within the organization. By doing this you find out if there is or is not a "values match," and employees develop a personally motivating reason for committing their energies to the organization.

THE POWER OF STORIES

One of the first things a professional speaker learns is the power of stories. Years after I have addressed an audience, one member will meet me somewhere else and immediately remember—not the statistics I used, or even the exact points I made—but the stories and real-life examples I used to drive a message home. People remember stories. People like stories. People learn from stories.

To communicate your values, tell stories. Use storytelling any time you can—in person at all meetings, in newsletters and on videotape to expose your audience to organizational values in action. Here are a few famous examples of organizational stories which clearly communicate corporate values:

Story #1

Ray Kroc, the founder and CEO of MacDonald's, was being driven past one of his fast-food outlets. He noticed there was litter strewn across the parking lot. Mr. Kroc immediately stopped his car, contacted the local manager, and (in his business suit) he and the manager picked up the trash.

Story #2

At General Electric Jack Welch had a special telephone installed in his office. He asked purchasing agents throughout the company to call him on that line whenever they cost-reduced a product. When a call came in, Mr. Welch stopped whatever else he was doing to answer the phone and personally congratulate the agent.

Story #3

A customer tried to return an automobile tire to Nordstrom's department store. "I'm so sorry," said the saleswoman, "but we do not sell tires at Nordstrom." "I know that I bought it here," insisted the customer. "Well, sir, we have never sold tires here," the clerk explained. "Do you happen to have your receipt?" "No," replied the customer, "but I know that I paid about $50 for the tire." "All right," said the saleswoman, "I'll take back the tire. Here is your $50 refund."

Story #4

Tom Melohn, the CEO of North American Tool and Die, gives out Superperson of the Month awards for the best contribution to the company's "zero defects" goal. But these awards aren't necessarily given out for task-oriented activities. Since one of North American Tool and Die's values is having a good time at work, Melohn once noticed an employee smiling and was pleased since this employee usually did not smile. Melohn asked another employee, who seemed to evoke the smile, "What did you say to her to get her to smile?" The employee replied, "Nothing. I just smiled at her." Melohn gave him $50 and the Superperson award—just for making someone else smile.

MANAGING BY "STORYING AROUND"

What follows is a detailed list of questions to ask yourself about incorporating stories in your management strategy:

- ○ What are the stories that you've heard about your company?

- ○ What are the stories that you tell or have told in the past?

- ○ What kind of stories might you want to start collecting and repeating?

- ○ What key point(s) are you looking for examples of?

○ Exactly where and how would it be advantageous to tell organizational stories?

If you already use stories, are you following these guidelines?

○ Do you always make sure the story is true? (Verify the facts.)

○ Do you always use the name of the hero/heroine of the story? (People like to hear their names or see them in print.)

○ Do you keep the story short and to the point? (Use the KISS—Keep It Simple, Stupid—method.)

○ Do you use words that help the listener form a mental picture? (Most long-term memory is stored in mental pictures.)

○ Do you frame the original and give it to the person or persons mentioned in the story? (People like a tangible expression of appreciation.)

MANAGING THE STRESS OF CONSTANT CHANGE

Just getting the job done isn't enough these days. Today's business environment demands more productivity and creativity from its workers at all levels. Especially for managers of constant change, one of the first ways to increase your productivity and creativity is to modify your response to stress.

Continual change brings continual pressure and stress. Poor responses to high-stress moments are the primary reason for mistakes, frustration and failure. It is possible to harness the difficulty of a stressful situation and turn it into a creative activity. Achieving grace under pressure not only allows you to deal creatively with the situation at hand, but also inspires those around you to stay calm and act effectively. Here is a simple method to take control of your body and mind under pressure:

Step One   *Focus on your breathing.* Instead of tensing up, which causes irregular breathing, consciously let yourself breathe smoothly, deeply and evenly.

Step Two   *Relax your face and smile.* Even the slightest smile may increase blood flow to the brain and help "reset" the nervous system so that it is less reactive to negative stress.

Step Three   *Keep an upright, balanced body position.* A balanced posture helps your body physically with stress by giving it room to breathe and preventing tension throughout the abdomen, back and neck.

Step Four   *Relax your muscles.* Muscle tension drains energy, slows reaction speed and clouds thinking processes.

Step Five   *Use your creative ability.* Think clearly. Refuse to hurry your response. Pause and restate the situation in terms that neither minimizes nor magnifies reality. Look for unique solutions.

With practice these steps become automatic responses. When your senses are alert, breathing is steady, posture is erect, emotions are controlled, and your mind is clear and looking for solutions. You are working in concert with your best management and problem-solving abilities.

LOWERING RESISTANCE TO CHANGE

Managers of change prepare to deal with resistance in several ways. First of all, they expect it. In the 16th century Nicolo Machiavelli said, "It must be remembered that there is nothing more difficult to plan, more doubtful of success, nor more dangerous to manage than the creation of new systems. For the initiator has the enmity of all who would profit by the preservation of the old and merely lukewarm defenders in those who would gain by the new one." By understanding and anticipating resistance, managers can greet it with an organized strategy:

Why people resist change: They think that management doesn't know how they feel.

Management strategy: Use questionnaires and focus groups to find out what people in the organization are thinking, what they believe the problems in the company are.

Why people resist change: They don't believe that change is necessary.

Management strategy: Point out and display the symptoms of inadequate performance that indicate the need for change. Create a consistent campaign with frequent notices on the bulletin board or in the company newsletter on global competitiveness. Print customer complaint letters or publish your successful competitor's price list. In the words of one manager, "We need to do a better job of 'selling the crisis.'" I believe that we also need to do a better job of selling the opportunities that the crisis affords.

Why people resist change: They are not prepared for it.

Management strategy: When it comes to change, no one likes surprises. Communicate early on about changes to come. Set the stage by helping people understand the concept of chaos, and how all businesses today are operating within this environment of uncertainty and turmoil. The more people understand about a situation—the alternatives and the consequences—the more likely they are to accept change.

Why people resist change: They think change is too risky.

Management strategy: All change contains elements of risk. It is often best to break change into small steps which have less risk, to propose change on a pilot basis or to let people know that change which proves unsuccessful can be reversed (if this is true). It is also important for people to understand the consequences of not changing—often the riskiest proposition of all.

Why people resist change:	They hear a lot about the importance of change, but don't see management doing anything differently.
Management strategy:	Make a list of those behavioral changes that you need to make your actions congruent with the change. Search out opportunities to "walk your talk." Remember, people will be watching to see if what you *do* aligns with what you *say*.
Why people resist change:	They do not have a clear picture of exactly what change will mean to them and their job functions on a daily basis.
Management strategy:	Make sure that you have told employees exactly what the change will mean in terms of organizational structure, job performance, training and compensation. Stress the interdependent relationship between the company's success and the employee's role, so everyone understands how they fit into the overall design.
Why people resist change:	They believe (and often rightly so) that change may cause them to lose their jobs.
Management strategy:	To turn insecurity into constructive tension, tell people the truth. Don't sugar-coat negativity—make sense of it. Listen to people's concerns and candidly validate or counter them with more realistic expectations. Clearly explain all possible ramifications (including possible job loss, if that is the case) so that they can make enlightened choices about their futures. Whatever the situation may be, don't lie to people. (My experience is that people in companies can deal with reality and facts much better than their managers often give them credit for.)

Why people resist change: They feel it is "your" change, not "mine."

Management strategy: Resistance will be less if participants have joined the diagnostic efforts leading them to agree on what the basic problems are. You can promote ownership by involving employees in the design and implementation of change.

Why people resist change: They think that management does not have their concerns at heart.

Management strategy: Help people accept change by being empathetic and directly addressing personal concerns. Have meetings during which employees can express concerns or fears, and offer suggestions for mak-ing change easier. When at all possible, position change as a "win-win" proposition by pointing out ways in which the individual as well as the organization will prosper with the change.

CHAPTER

5

Doing Business Internationally

> **❝***Mistakes of corporate representatives because of language or intercultural incompetence can jeopardize millions of dollars in negotiations and purchases, sales and contracts, as well as undermine customer relations.***❞**
>
> —Philip Harris and Robert Moran, Authors
> *Managing Cultural Differences*

> **❝***There are two basic 'working' rules: First, learn the language. Second, don't jump to conclusions.***❞**
>
> —John Mole, Author
> *Mind Your Manners: Cultural Clash in the European Single Market*

CULTURAL AWARENESS

Never touch the head of a Thai—even a child—or pass an object over it. (The head is considered sacred in Thailand.) Use formal titles with the French until you've known them for a considerable length of time. (The quick familiarity of Americans can be offensive to the French.) Offer a gift when invited to a Japanese home. (Gifts must not be lavish, but in good taste and nicely wrapped. Don't use white wrapping paper, however; it's a sign of death.) Be sure to provide plenty of background information when working with a German. (The Germans have a saying, "You have to start with Charlemagne," which means they require detail and a historical perspective on issues before making decisions.) Don't be surprised if your Saudi counterpart shows up for a business appointment a day late. (Time does not have the same meaning or cultural value in Saudi Arabia as it does in the United States.)

Why bother with all of this? Because respecting another culture and its etiquette and customs isn't simply good manners. It's good business.

While many business people focus on the functional skills needed for international negotiations, they may overlook the importance of cultural savvy. The technical abilities of professionals are certainly important, but without a proper understanding of cultural norms, even the most skilled technician may make social blunders which can jeopardize business opportunities.

It's both dangerous and ill-advised to go into the international workplace with the mistaken impression that "business is business" all over the world. The bottom line is that what works best in domestic situations may not apply abroad.

An American executive in France invited his entire office staff to his apartment in a chic section of Paris. Everyone felt uncomfortable, and the discomfort continued at the office following the party. It took him weeks to discover that in France it is considered inappropriate for executives to socialize with secretaries and other office workers.

The cultural differences that have to be taken into account may turn out to be as important as a contrasting set of values that determine the focal point of negotiating objectives, or as trivial as behavioral mannerisms that subtly block your ability to establish confidence and trust.

"One of Canada's leading banks invited a Chinese delegation for dinner. The Canadian host chose to share his hosting responsibilities with a colleague.

"The dinner was not a success. Both the Chinese and the Canadians remained relatively uneasy throughout the meal. During the dinner, no welcoming speeches or toast to mutual good health were made. At the end of the meal, the Chinese stood up, thanked the bank officials, declined a ride back to their hotel, and left feeling slighted.

"The Canadians also felt upset. They found the departure of the Chinese to be very abrupt, yet they did not know what they had done wrong. Despite planning the menu carefully (avoiding such foods as beef and dairy products), providing excellent translation services, and extending normal Canadian courtesies, the Canadians knew something had gone wrong; they were worried and somewhat hurt by the lack of rapport.

"When the situation was analyzed, it was clear that the Chinese expectations had not been fulfilled. First, having two people share hosting responsibilities was confusing to the hierarchically minded Chinese. Second, because age is viewed as an indication of seniority, the Chinese considered the youth of their Canadian hosts as a slight to their own status. Third, in China, it is traditional for the host to offer a welcoming toast at the beginning of the meal, which is then reciprocated by the guests; by not doing so, the Canadians were thought rude.

"The Canadians' lack of understanding of the hierarchical nature of Chinese society and the Chinese ways of showing respect clearly cost them in their business dealings with the visiting delegation."

From the book *Culture's Consequences: International Differences in Work Related Values.*

The thing to keep in mind is that although the international business environment may blur distinctions between some cultures, it hasn't eliminated them completely. Even representatives from different parts of the European Community still encounter—and stumble over—differences in cultural style. When the prototypical reserved British business person confronts the machismo of the Latins or interacts with the argumentative French, there is still potential for cultural clash. And no region of the world has greater variety and diversity of languages, races and religions than Asia, although the cultures of the countries of Asia and the Pacific have crisscrossed and intermingled for centuries. There is still much cultural variance in the world.

There are many ways to show cultural awareness and respect. Take this example from the book *Do's and Taboos Around the World*, edited by Roger Axtell: A U.S. doctor of public health recently back from West Africa offers an example of how important it is to work within the culture you are visiting. "I don't just pop over and start handing out anti-malaria pills on the corner," she says. "First I visit with the village chief. After he gives his blessing, I move in with the local witch doctor. After she shows me her techniques and I show her mine—and a few lives are saved—maybe then we can get the first native to swallow the first pill."

One basic way for business professionals to honor a culture is to learn to speak the language of the country you'll be dealing with. Speaking a foreign language can be an important business strategy (and one that is utilized by too few American executives and negotiators). Speaking in the appropriate foreign language, no matter how rudimentary your skill, is almost always received favorably—as a sign that you truly want to understand the culture.

However, even if you are multilingual, it is still only the tip of the intercultural iceberg. Language learning without cultural awareness is labor lost. If you don't know anything about the culture you're dealing with, even though you speak the language like a native, you're still at a disadvantage.

CULTURAL BARRIERS

By far the biggest potential barrier to international business dealings comes in the form of cultural differences. Culture is, basically, a set of shared values that a group of people hold. Such values affect how you think and behave and, more importantly, the kind of criteria by which you judge others. Shared cultural norms give people a sense of common identity and a means of relating to each other. Culture has both explicit rules and implicit, unrecognized sets of underlying meanings through which experience is interpreted. Cultural meanings render some forms of activity as normal and right and others strange or wrong.

A CASE IN POINT

Take this scene in a Chinese cemetery. Watching a Chinese reverently placing fresh fruit on a grave, an American visitor asked, "When do you expect your ancestors to get up and eat the fruit?" The Chinese replied, "As soon as your ancestors get up and smell the flowers."

All of us, without training or extensive exposure to people different from ourselves, act appropriately within our own cultural context and make assumptions that everyone we meet shares the same basic values and priorities. Too often the interpretation made is that the person who is different is wrong, deficient or lacking in character—depending on the nature of the particular incident.

A necessary first step to cultural sensitivity is to eliminate useless labels of "right" and "wrong." Cultures are not right or wrong, better or worse; they are just different.

Swedish expatriate managers often do not have the opportunity to explain their desire for balancing professional and private life to their foreign colleagues. Swedes frequently surprise their international clients when they expect work to end at 5:00 P.M. on Friday or when they announce their intention to return home at the end of the day on the first plane in order to spend more time with their families. According to Swedish business people, many foreigners, especially Americans, are willing to work all evening and all weekend to finish an important project; they frequently judge a Swede's behavior as demonstrating an inadequate commitment to work and quickly become annoyed. In actuality the Swedes are simply demonstrating their strong commitment to quality of life, whereas the Americans and other similar foreigners behave according to their strong commitment to task.

From the book *International Dimensions of Organizational Behavior.*

Each culture has rules for behavior and living which its members take for granted. Few of us are aware of our own cultural behaviors and biases because cultural imprinting is begun at a very early age, and while some of culture's knowledge, rules, beliefs, values, phobias and anxieties are taught explicitly, most of it is absorbed subconsciously. However, by becoming more aware of our unique cultural traits, and examining the impact they have on our thinking and behavior, we can become more sensitive to others.

You can begin your preparations for whatever country you're doing business with by listing the basic assumptions of doing business in your own culture. A list of business attitudes and assumptions that prevail in the United States and the corresponding value they represent might include things like "the squeaky wheel gets the grease" (aggressiveness), "God helps those who help themselves" (initiative), "time is money" (time thriftiness), "get right to the point" (directness), "no rest for the wicked" (work ethic), and "everyone is motivated by money" (monetary motivation).

The object is to make your own list and then examine how these might be different in your destination country. (Just understanding that these are not necessarily universally held concepts is helpful.) Next, make a list of typical working situations you'll find yourself in and examine how you might have to adjust.

A CASE IN POINT

Researchers say that a common cultural mistake is an American's assumption that people from other cultures appreciate our informal way of addressing one another. In the U.S. people address each other by first names right after being introduced. But in France it may take three to six months before business associates feel comfortable without a formal title.

To most Europeans, the informality and casualness that typify the American social interactions look phoney and gratuitous. We may interpret European formality as stiff and unfriendly.

Aside from cultural traits, each of us brings along personal traits which may enhance or hinder working abroad. (If you are naturally impatient, you will not thrive in China, say, or Latin America.) By reflecting on personal characteristics and seeing how they might work against you internationally, you can strategize how to remove potential stumbling blocks.

How Others See Us

A recent study queried employees from around the world who were currently working or conducting business dealings with Americans. The researchers wanted to know how people from different cultures viewed their U.S. counterparts. Here is a list of attributes (stereotypes) that were most often applied to Americans:

- ○ Get down to business.
- ○ Offensively informal.
- ○ Win-lose negotiators.
- ○ In a hurry—never allow themselves to enjoy life.
- ○ Disrespectful of authority.
- ○ Follow rules.
- ○ Talk too much—hate silence—poor listeners.
- ○ Look to contract, not relationship.
- ○ Outgoing, friendly, generous, wealthy.
- ○ Loud, rude, boastful, immature.
- ○ Hard-working.
- ○ Extravagant, wasteful.
- ○ Confident they have all the answers.
- ○ Ignorant of other countries.
- ○ Lack class consciousness.
- ○ Racially prejudiced.

It is also widely believed that American women are promiscuous.

CROSS-CULTURAL BUSINESS STYLES

There are very real differences in the cultures and business customs in every land outside your home country. While many areas of cross-cultural differences need to be considered by business people embarking on foreign ventures—and the main skill to learn is to stay mentally alert and flexible—the following simplified list will give you a starting point for evaluating these differences. As you read through these cultural traits, see if you can ascertain which ones are inherent in your culture and which represent other cultures with which you come into contact.

Confrontation vs. Consensus   Cultures will differ in whether they favor candor above consensus. In some cultures conflict and confrontation are not only acceptable, they are desirable. In others people avoid criticism at all costs in order to allow everyone to "save face."

The Group vs. the Individual   There is an emphasis on strong individualism— a sense of being unique, an expected need for personal fulfillment—that permeates some cultures. Other cultures promote individuals who seek their identity and sense of fulfillment within the spectrum of the group.

Concept of Time   Cultures value and relate to time differently. One culture might view time as a commodity to "save" or to "waste" while another looks at time as a constant flow which cannot be contained or controlled.

Concept of Space   The comfort level of different cultures varies when it comes to physical space separating participants. Some cultures compress the space between people and even touch each other (lightly gripping another's arm, touching the lapel of another's jacket, or sometimes briefly hugging) during business dealings. Other cultures formally distance themselves from one another when doing business, getting close only to shake hands or to exchange business cards.

Decision Making   Some groups believe that only quantifiable data is real information, and will make decisions on "hard facts" or "pure numbers" only. In contrast, insight and intuition, especially when handed down from someone of high regard, is given enormous value in many cultures when important business decisions are being made.

Contracts and Agreements   In some cultures personal bonds and the spoken word are far more binding than the written contract. In others the meticulous wording of legal documents is viewed as paramount.

Personal Relationships in Business   In some cultures interpersonal relationships are pivotal to doing business. In those cases one must deal with business partners face-to-face (relying on telephone calls or written communication alone is meaningless) and establish an ongoing presence by building long-term relationships. Other cultures disregard much of the personal side of business and focus primarily on selling and persuading others with the facts of the business arrangement.

Manifestations of Power and Status   In some cultures power and status are obviously displayed in possessions (large office, expensive automobile, ornate jewelry, designer clothing, etc.). In other cultures external manifestations of organizational power and status (like office space) are more uniformly distributed, and overt displays of status are discouraged.

It is also helpful to know how different cultures define status. Is it by the academic degrees held, by social level, by job title, by knowledge or skill possessed, by personal contacts or by the school graduated from?

Loyalty   In some cultures it is expected that individuals in companies will be loyal foremost to themselves. In other cultures loyalty to the organization is primary. In still other cultures loyalty to the family or clan may take precedence over all other loyalties. (In the latter case it is seen as grossly disloyal *not* to favor relatives and friends in business dealings.)

Problem Solving   One culture may stress the solving of problems by deduction, beginning first with premises or stated principles. Others will stress an inductive approach in which conclusions are stated first, followed by an explanation of how the conclusions were arrived at.

Locus of Control   Some cultures display a strong belief that individuals have control over the events in their lives, that they are personally responsible for outcomes. Other cultures seem to believe that results are under the influence of external forces—change, luck, fate—and that individuals have limited control.

Deference to Authority   Cultures differ in their deference to authority figures in an organization. Some show respect for title and position in a hierarchy, while other cultures ignore, challenge or treat people in power as a liability.

Formality vs. Informality   Proper use of names and titles is often a source of confusion in international business relations. In some cultures it is appropriate to use titles until use of the first name is suggested. While some cultures promote first name interaction between business associates from the first meeting, first names are seldom used at all in the business dealings of other cultures.

Negotiation Styles   Negotiation styles vary widely from country to country. Some cultures are conflict-oriented, with each party trying to put his or her opponent on the defensive; some cultures argue vehemently over every trivial point; some cultures use a wide range of visible emotions as part of their negotiation style; and some cultures depend on consensus and meeting the needs of everyone.

Researchers studying intercultural differences find that cultural values even effect cognition. A recent article in *The Journal of Business Communication* states: "Cognition as a human faculty is probably shared by all people across cultures, but cognitive frames cannot be assumed to be identical in all cultures. The dominant values of a society, its ideologies, and its ways of looking at the world around it affect the nature, scope, and definitions of rationality and of the inquiry by researchers in that society. What is rational and logical thus apparently differs among cultures and countries because world views or perceptions differ radically among people around the globe."

It can be helpful to remember that just when you think you are being the most reasonable and logical, and what you are trying to explain is self-evident, you may sound unreasonable and highly illogical to others.

Author's note—I do not mean to imply that every person within a certain culture will behave in identical ways. Understanding cultural stereotyping is by no means ironclad and cannot be extended to the individual level. In reality, no two people belonging to the same culture are going to respond in exactly the same way. The spectrum of human behavior can be found in any given culture. However, cultural stereotypes are valid to the extent that they provide clues on what to expect *generally* when meeting and dealing with members of that culture.

INTERNATIONAL BUSINESS PRACTICES

With the growing internationalization of corporate operations, business people increasingly require some knowledge of what is recognized as normal business practice in other countries. All business people are encouraged to become business diplomats who make an effort to understand and appreciate the differences in other countries.

Even when there are apparent similarities of peoples in geographic regions, cultural differences may require alteration of strategic market planning. North American companies and unions discovered this in Canada when they tried to treat their operations there as mere United States extensions. Europeans realized this in Bolivia and Argentina, where a common cultural heritage is layered by political and social conditions.

The biggest change for the U.S. in the international marketplace is that today foreign businesses are insisting that we become sensitive to their ways. Executives who try to negotiate or sell or even interact without that sensitivity will undoubtedly lose business opportunities and money. We must remember that in our global dealings we may be separated from our international counterparts not only by physical features, different languages and business etiquette, but also by different ways of perceiving the world, defining business goals, expressing thoughts and feelings, showing or hiding motivations and interests.

Frankness and directness, virtues for Americans, are not desirous to Mexicans in formal encounters nor to Japanese at any time. Americans and Germans are more likely to start out trusting the other party until proven wrong, while in Latin America people would be inclined to mistrust until good faith is proven. American humor is often seen as strange and inappropriate by members of other cultures, while the Japanese art of being overly humble and apologetic seems condescending and artificial to many in the West.

Longtime residents of Japan have a saying: "If you have been doing business in Japan for six months, you think you know all about the system. But if you've lived in Japan for six years, you realize that you are just beginning to understand the system."

In the *Asian Wall Street Journal* an article appeared commenting on Eastman Kodak Japan Ltd.'s decision to downsize its Japanese work force. The article stated these facts: On February 2, 1993, Kodak announced that it would lay off two-thirds of the R&D staff at its high-technology research laboratory in Yokaham, about seventy people. This action was coming just three years after Kodak opened the multimillion-dollar technical center, built as a symbol of Kodak's long-term commitment to the huge and strategically important Japanese market. The article editorialized, "Although the layoffs are small-scale when one considers that Kodak's Japan operations employ thousands of people, and that Kodak has said it will reduce its staff by 2000 people world-wide, they represent a complete reversal of the strategy Kodak articulated to its work force and the Japanese public. To add to the company's woes, the week before the layoff announcement Kodak had canceled its employment offers to eight Japanese university students. (In Japan, the school year ends in March, and graduates join their new employer on the first working day of April.) Some of these students attend Japan's most prestigious universities.

By canceling its offers of employment, Kodak has shot itself in both feet. Kodak will not be a credible recruiter or employer for a very long time in Japan. A Japanese investment banker was quoted as saying that Kodak should cut costs even further by shutting down all operations in Japan since they have told their current and prospective employees that they are not trustworthy as an employer. 'Kodak should cut costs further because they have no future in Japan.' "

For foreign companies in Japan, the lesson is clear: you cannot do business there if you don't do business according to acceptable Japanese business practices. The labor environment is unlike that in New York or Düsseldorf. In Asia, and most especially in Japan, there is a trend toward paternalistic governments which, reasonably enough, expect multinationals operating in their lands to demonstrate a commitment to the social and national aspirations. The decision to reduce the number of permanent Japanese employees may not only severely affect a company's ability to recruit Japanese nationals in the future, it may actually threaten its continued existence.

RELIGIOUS BELIEFS AND CUSTOMS

Religious beliefs and traditional customs are some of the best examples of what a businessperson must come to grips with when doing business in some countries. One of the strangest beliefs for many Westerners to accept is the superstition that permeates the everyday lives of Asians and serious Asian business practice.

The Chinese are well known for their strict observance of a bewildering assortment of "dos" and "don'ts," perhaps the most universal of which is *fung shui*—the positive or negative juxtapositioning of the elements of wind and water. For example, the Chinese name for the Hong Kong area of Kowloon means "nine dragons" and is derived from the nine hills that rise behind the densely populated industrial and residential area of the Kowloon peninsula. According to Chinese superstition it is fatal to disturb a dragon, and while erecting an office block or housing complex, the *fung shui* expert might advise a halt to construction because you are building in the dragon's eye. A *fung shui* expert is also commonly called in when a company sets up a new office to advise on the most auspicious positioning of furniture, the most auspicious colors to choose, etc.

If, by some chance, a building is erected on what is seen by the Chinese as an unlucky site, in order to ensure the peace of mind of your local staff, it is a good idea to employ the services of a priest to carry out an exorcism ceremony. In this way you rid the property of evil spirits and ensure the success and prosperity of your company.

If you doubt that this is very serious business practice, just look at the cost companies are willing to pay to ensure good luck. The rate for a good *fung shui* man to check out a building site or design can be as much as $250,000.

A CASE IN POINT

The Hongkong Land Company Ltd., one of the world's largest property companies, built Exchange Square, the home of the Unified Stock Exchange. It was designed and constructed for good *fung shui*. For example, the skylight in the roof of The Rotunda was designed not merely to give sunlight to the trees in the lobby, but rather to allow good fortune and good spirits to pour in through the skylight and down into the Stock Exchange.

While superstition is perhaps an extreme example of the cultural differences that exist in societies, there are many other deeply rooted customs in each country that can become a veritable minefield for the unwary business visitor or for the company setting up business there. Therefore, awareness, sensitivity, tolerance and respect for the customs of the country you are planning to do business in are absolutely imperative.

PREPARING FOR THE INTERNATIONAL BUSINESS TRIP

The Business Council for International Understanding estimates that international personnel who go abroad without cross-cultural preparation have a failure rate ranging from 33–66 percent in contrast to less than 2 percent of those who had the benefit of such training. While not at all comprehensive, the following list is the minimum information that a foreigner should have about the business practices in a host country before going there:

1. **Greeting Behaviors**

    ○ How do business people greet one another? Do they touch or shake hands? If so, do they prefer a firm or a gentle grip? Do they bow?

    ○ When should business cards be exchanged? How should cards be handled?

    ○ How are introductions made?

    ○ What is considered good manners for greeting senior executives when they enter a room?

    ○ How are you expected to address others?

A CASE IN POINT

An American traveled nine thousand miles to meet his clients in Singapore. On the trip over he memorized the names of all the key men he was to see. This was no easy job, as each man had three names. The board chairman was Lo Win Hao, and the American began his greetings by addressing him as Mr. Hao, only to be told by a colleague that he had been too friendly and informal much too soon. In Chinese the surname comes first and the given name last. It was as if he was calling his clients Mr. Bob or Mr. John.

2. Business Protocol

○ How formal and ritualistic is this culture in their approach to business dealings?

○ What is the culture's concept of time? How important is it to be prompt for a business meeting? What does it mean when/if you are left waiting at an appointment?

○ What is the protocol for seating around the conference table?

○ How much space between people in normal business situations is their "comfort zone"?

○ What is the communication style of the people in the host country?

○ How much time should be spent in pleasantries and social interaction? Who takes the initiative in "getting down to business"?

○ How do you go about obtaining information?

○ When is the use of humor appropriate?

○ What topics of conversation are considered inappropriate or unprofessional?

○ If you are a female (or a minority) in business, how should you expect to be treated?

○ How are males and females expected to interact in business situations?

○ In what language will the meeting take place? Do you need to have translated handouts or other business materials? Do you need an interpreter?

○ How much physical contact is appropriate?

○ What is appropriate behavior when leaving and saying good-bye?

A CASE IN POINT

"The most important thing I learned on my international assignment was not to rush meetings with the typical 'American take-charge attitude.' I was present when a newly arrived officer chief was taken by the outgoing chief to meet a key contact. The hand-off was so important that I had travelled some distance to be present. The incumbent and I watched, helpless and horrified, as the new man destroyed in five seconds what the incumbent had taken a year to build. Undoubtedly the new man thought he was creating the impact of the hard-charging young executive, but in reality he was tearing down a delicate relationship."

Major, U.S. Air Force.

3. Negotiating Behaviors

○ How important is it to create an ambience of good feelings and harmony? How important is it for people within this culture to like the people with whom they are doing business?

○ How do negotiators reach decisions? Who negotiates? Is negotiating done by an individual or a team? Will their negotiators have the authority to make a firm decision?

○ Are business deals made verbally or by contract?

○ How direct can you be when dealing with this culture?

○ Is a deadline always a deadline—or should it be considered only a flexible guideline?

○ What is the negotiation style of people in this culture—do they have a fallback position, expect the other party to reveal their own interests and priorities first, enjoy the fine art of haggling, or look for a compromise position? Do they spend a great deal of time on the emotional and dramatic effects of negotiating or do they rely on a strictly logical approach? Are they likely to use a sense of obligation as part of their negotiation tactics?

- Is asking questions a primary bargaining strategy or is questioning interpreted as prying and inappropriately nosy?

- Are decisions made primarily on a cost-benefit basis or on the basis of saving someone from embarrassment?

- How does this culture use silence in the negotiating process?

- How do they feel about lawyers attending the negotiations?

A CASE IN POINT

Ford Motor Company, when Lee Iacocca was running it, wanted to buy Ferrari. Some of Iacocca's top people went to see Enzo Ferrari and they came to an understanding: Ford would acquire not the race car but the production side of the company so that the Ferrari name could be used in the United States. The deal was made on handshakes between gentlemen. Soon, though, Ford's attorneys arrived in Italy with contracts, and a crew arrived to take inventory. This was normal business procedure for the Americans, but Ferrari was disgruntled—to his thinking he had an understanding with a gentleman, not with a group of attorneys and accountants—and had second thoughts. The deal fell through. In the end Fiat stepped in and gave Ferrari the money he needed.

From the book *Going International,* by Lennie Copeland and Lewis Griggs.

4. Social Behavior

- How much socializing is not only expected, but necessary for doing your job successfully?

- How much importance will be placed on the existence of and adherence to rules for social behavior?

- How do people organize their daily activities? What is the normal meal schedule? Is there a daytime rest period?

○ Is it typical to be invited to a private home for dinner? If so, how are you expected to reciprocate? If you are invited for dinner, should you arrive early, on time or late? If late—how late?

○ Are dinner or lunch meetings most desirable?

○ Does one drink or not at a business meal? Are you expected to offer a formal toast before drinking?

○ What is the proper seating order at a restaurant or dinner table?

○ Are females and/or spouses included in after-hours business entertainment?

○ What are considered good table manners?

○ Is it expected practice to exchange gifts? If so, what kinds of gifts are proper and how should they be presented?

○ What kind of compliments are expected, and which are inappropriate?

A woman traveling in the Middle East as chief emissary for her Fortune 500 corporation was surprised after meeting with men all day to be placed at a separate table with their wives at dinner.

5. Nonverbal Communication

○ What meaning is attached to physical gestures in the host's culture?

○ What does it mean to make eye contact, to use hand and arm gestures, to smile, to laugh, to cross your legs, to put your hands in your pockets or on your hips, to touch another person, etc.?

○ Especially—what gestures are absolutely taboo in this culture? (An example would be the "thumbs up" gesture that North Americans and many other cultures flash when they want to signify "Good job!" or "Well done!" In certain locales, that gesture is considered offensive and should be avoided.)

An American in Greece had five products to sell, so to drive home a point, he held up his hand with five fingers outstretched, his palm facing his Greek customer. In Greece the gesture is considered obscene and thus could stand in the way of the deal being completed.

Of course it could have been worse. If he had held up two hands, the gesture would have been doubly obscene, and the sale would have been as good as dead.

6. Dress and Grooming

○ How should you dress for professional purposes? Are short or long-sleeved shirts required? Can suit jackets ever be removed?

○ Is jewelry out of place? Sunglasses?

○ When you are off work, are jeans, slacks or shorts ever acceptable? If so—on what occasions?

○ What is considered professional grooming when it comes to haircuts, hair styles and facial hair?

A business woman in Togo bought some beautiful beads. What she didn't know was that locally, the beads were not worn at the neck, but rather at the waist to hold up a sort of loincloth under the skirt. The woman made an entrance wearing around her neck what to every Togolese eye was part of a pair of underpants.

7. Religion, Morals, Superstitions

○ What are the strong traditions that this culture has which govern daily life and social interactions?

○ What are the religious beliefs and moral attitudes of this culture?

○ What are the business ethics of this culture?

○ What social behaviors are out of place (smoking, drinking, gambling, etc.)?

○ What special religious or superstitious customs dominate business practices? How are you expected to behave when others observe their religious customs?

"What do you do when you've been asked to dinner by your Moslem host and (in the middle of the meal) he takes out his prayer rug to pray? Well, they hadn't covered that in my pre-assignment training, so I was bewildered . . . do I stop eating, bow my head, what? Luckily, I was not the only guest, so I followed the lead of others, who quietly continued talking and eating until our host returned to the dinner party."

Expatriate Executive.

In addition to the preparations listed above, I suggest doing some background readings on the host country—its history, fine arts, native sports, political, social and economic structure, etc. What is the status of business? How does the culture view foreigners? Who are their national heroes? What is the religious history? What kind of local transportation is available? What are the important holidays and how are they observed? Can you recognize their national anthem?

The more in depth your knowledge of local culture, the more you'll understand not just the "what" and the "where" but also the "why" behind it.

Then, when meeting foreigners, show your interest in the things that interest them. If you are sincere, it may be very good business to mention to a German that you've been reading Goethe, or to visit a historic temple in Japan, or to ask a Brit about cricket.

I've also noticed that the rest of the world takes a keen interest in global affairs. Before you leave on a business trip, it is wise to keep up with current events internationally so that you can comment on them in conversation. (Subscribe to the *Economist* or the *International Herald Tribune,* or read any periodical with broad international coverage.)

It is not necessary to adopt other people's cultural norms as part of your own personal value system. What is required, however, is to identify, understand, accept and respect other cultures and try to understand how your behavior may impact them.

SKILLS FOR INTERNATIONAL NEGOTIATORS

Pierre Casse, lecturer in the Economic Development Institute at the World Bank, stated that international negotiators need five skills. Paraphrased somewhat, these skills make a useful list for our review as global businesspeople:

- ○ To be able to see the world as other people see it and to understand others' behavior from their perspective.

- ○ To be able to demonstrate the advantages of one's own perspective so that international counterparts in business will be willing to consider it.

- ○ To be able to manage stress and cope with ambiguous situations as well as unpredictable demands.

- ○ To be able to express one's ideas so that people one deals with will accurately understand.

- ○ To be sensitive to the cultural background of the others and adjust the suggestions one makes to the existing constraints and limitations.

THE LITTLE THINGS

Even if your professional business presentation has been perfected and your cultural skills sharpened, it might be the nonbusiness part of your preparation—the seemingly inconsequential, commonsense travel issues—that get you into trouble. On one occasion I had scheduled a business trip to Hong Kong during the week preceding Easter. I arrived to find that many business people were out of town that week. Monday was a Chinese holiday honoring the dead, and Friday and the next Monday were Easter holidays, so most executives were taking a ten-day vacation. Needless to say, it was not my most productive trip.

Here are a few of the "little things" that almost ruined the business dealings of other international travelers:

> "I didn't allow a free day before the business meeting started to get over the effects of jet lag, so when I was supposed to give my presentation at 8:00 A.M. the morning after I arrived in Singapore, I was exhausted."
>
> —Salesman for an international firm

> "I didn't bring a converter for my U.S. hairdryer, and I still had wet hair when I met my business partners in Germany. Believe me, that was not the professional image that I wanted to project."
>
> —Female entrepreneur

> "The traffic situation was so bad in Bangkok that it was impossible to get to more than one appointment each morning. Not knowing that in advance, I'd overbooked myself and consequently missed several important meetings."
>
> —Software company executive

> "I didn't know that the coffee they served in Europe was so strong. By my third cup, I was 'wired.'"
>
> —International conference attendee

> "I complimented a distinguished English gentleman on the knickers he was wearing, only to find out later that in Britain knee-length trousers are called 'plus fours,' while 'knickers' are ladies' underpants."
>
> —General Manager of international division

"I arrived in Beijing and was sent back to the United States because my visa was for the Republic of China (Taiwan) and not the People's Republic of China. The U.S. ticketing agent had not noticed, and so I had been allowed to board the plane. But, believe me, they noticed in the PRC."

—American Executive

"I won't bore you with the tedious details, but just believe me when I say that I've found out there are two kinds of luggage: carry-on and lost!"

—International salesman

Global Communication

The language that a man speaks governs his view of reality;
it determines his perception of the world. The picture of
the universe shifts from tongue to tongue.

—David Thompson, Author
Language

Polish people are irrational, sensitive, and emotional. You have to
appeal to these qualities in your marketing.

—Mariola Czechowska, Warsaw Managing Director
Young and Rubicam

THE MESSAGE IS THE MESSAGE RECEIVED

Two psychiatrists meet in the street one day. One psychiatrist says to the other, "How are you?" The second psychiatrist nods, walks hurriedly on and thinks, "I wonder what he meant by that?"

When people communicate with one another, they make certain assumptions about the process of perceiving, judging, and thinking and the reasoning patterns of each other. They make these assumptions without even realizing they are making them. When two people communicate, they seldom get identical impressions from the interchange.

If communicating person to person can be so difficult, then communicating across cultures is the most difficult of all. Effective meaning is flavored by each person's own cognitive world and cultural understanding, and effects of cultural conditioning are so pervasive that people whose experience has been limited to the rules of one culture have difficulty understanding communication based on another set of rules.

The best way to understand intercultural communication is to focus on the role of decoding and perception in the communication process. This is because, in intercultural communication, decoding by the receiver of signals is subject to social values and cultural variables not necessarily present in the sender. A sender may transmit unconscious or unintentional signals along with the intended message, which may enhance or obscure it to the extent that the intended message may not be picked up at all by the receiver. The receiver sorts through various signals, paying attention to some and attaching meanings that are culturally determined.

Perception is at the heart of intercultural communication. We misperceive and misunderstand each other all the time, even when we share the same values and culture. It just makes good sense that the process gets more complicated when we are communicating with those whose values and culture differ.

Sending a message is not communication. There is no communication until the receiver has perceived and retained the message. (In other words, your sending the signal doesn't mean anything until the other party picks it up and understands it.) Therefore, the barriers to communication can best be lowered by addressing the cultural factors that influence interpretation and by being sincerely empathetic—putting yourself into the position of the other person and trying to view things through his or her eyes.

A CASE IN POINT

As an international communicator, you should assume that your audiences need assistance interpreting what may be "common knowledge" to you. A good example of this kind of assistance was in an article geared to readers of an English newspaper in Japan. It went like this: ". . . the high school textbooks are scheduled to go into use next April, when the school year begins."

The Japanese writer of the article put himself in the shoes of his readers from other countries in which the school year does not always start in April, even though it would have sounded redundant to locals.

When communicating across cultures, attention should be paid to the following possibilities:

○ The receiver of your message may not interpret the words you used in the same way as you intended.

○ The receiver of your message may pick up on other signals (tone of voice, facial expression, body movement, etc.) which obscure your original message.

○ The receiver of your message may not know as much about the topic as you.

○ And, when you are the receiver, be aware that the sender of the message may have given another meaning to the words which is quite different from your interpretation, and consider the fact that you may have picked up on unintended signals which are obscuring the intended message.

COMMUNICATING WITHOUT SAYING A WORD

People around the world use gestures or body movement to convey specific messages. Though countries sometimes use the same gestures, they often have different meanings. Waving "good-bye" with the whole hand side to side (the way we do it in America) means "no" throughout most of Europe. In Peru that gesture means "Come here." Called the *moutza* in Greece, that same gesture is a serious insult, and the closer the hand to the other person's face, the more threatening it is considered to be.

Even the "OK" sign commonly used in the United States as signifying approval is a gesture that has several different meanings according to the country. In France it means zero; in Japan it is a symbol for money; and in Brazil it carries a vulgar connotation.

As a foreigner abroad, you can get into trouble even before you open your mouth to speak. Body language, facial expressions, gestures, table manners, gift-giving and how (or if) you initiate physical contact are an important part of international communication. Here are a few basic examples:

○ If you are taking flowers as a business gift—in France chrysanthemums are appropriate only for funerals, and in Germany red roses are reserved for lovers.

○ The average German doesn't smile during business situations. The average American smiles often (which may be seen as misplaced frivolity).

○ A nod means "no" in Bulgaria, and shaking the head side-to-side means "yes."

○ When in Latin America, don't keep eyeing your watch. Among Hispanics time is a casual, even vague concept.

○ It is an insult to point the sole of your shoe at a person in Egypt, Saudi Arabia, Singapore and Thailand.

○ If you stand with your hands on your hips in Mexico, it is seen as a threatening posture.

○ If you have a conversation with your hands in your pockets, it is considered bad manners in France, Belgium, Finland and Sweden.

○ If you are invited to a business dinner at a private home, be very prompt in Germany and Denmark, arrive fifteen to twenty minutes late in Mexico or England, and come up to one hour late in Italy or Spain.

○ Never give someone in China a gift of a clock because the Chinese characters for the word "clock" sound similar to those for "funeral," so it might be implied that you are giving a gift of death.

○ In France, where cooking is an esteemed art, it is rude to salt food, and bread is torn, not sliced off the loaf.

○ In Hong Kong smoking is a beloved hobby. Don't be surprised when folks light up between courses at a formal dinner.

○ In different countries an effusive host may present you with the specialty of that region. In Finland it may be a slice of raw reindeer meat, in China a 1,000-year-old egg (actually only about ten weeks old, but still odiferous), in England it will be organ meats—sweetbreads and the like. Even if you are not hungry, you should taste whatever is offered. It is a tiny, symbolic gesture of understanding and respect.

○ In Japan a nod of the head does not necessarily imply agreement. It usually means that the listener has understood the message.

○ In Indonesia handshaking with either sex is perfectly acceptable, but using the left hand for this purpose is strictly "taboo."

○ In the United Kingdom (and especially in London) physical image is very important. Business people dress formally and conservatively. It is not the place to try out a flashy "new look."

○ In Japan your business cards are your identity. They must be printed in your own and in the host country's language. In business meetings you pass them out to your counterparts in order of seniority. When handed a card by a Japanese counterpart, study it before respectfully stowing it among your belongings. If you casually disregard the business cards of others—or bend, fold, spindle or mutilate them— it is considered poor manners and very bad business.

INTERNATIONAL COMMUNICATION

The challenge for international business communication has never been greater. Worldwide business organizations have discovered that intercultural communication is a subject of importance not just because they have to deal increasingly with foreigners, but also because the work force of the future within their own national borders is growing more and more diverse, ethnically and culturally.

A CASE IN POINT

Much to the surprise of a Magnavox representative at a London meeting, when he suggested "tabling" the next item on the agenda, his host immediately began to discuss it. To the British the verb turns out to have the opposite meaning than it does to the Americans.

Although obvious cultural differences certainly exist among western societies—particularly in European and South American countries—the greatest challenges to communication may come in the myriad of cultural differences we encounter when organizations expand throughout the Asia-Pacific region. General Electric's CEO, Jack Welch, sees the future of global expansion as getting increasingly difficult. He says, "The expansion into Europe was comparatively easy from a cultural standpoint. As Japan developed, the cultural differences were larger, and U.S. business has had more difficulties there. As we look ahead, the cultural challenges will be larger still in the rest of Asia—from China to Indonesia to Thailand to India—where more than half the world lives. U.S. companies will have to adapt to those cultures if they are to succeed in the 21st century."

In general, what is needed are global communicators who are knowledgeable about and sensitive to cross-cultural nuances. The role of global communications is to create strategies that proclaim the corporate vision globally, discuss cultural differences in employees (both intranationally and from country to country), and find ways to adapt to and take advantage of this global diversity.

A CASE IN POINT

At a meeting in Singapore recently, representatives from an American manufacturing organization were negotiating a business arrangement with their Asian counterparts. Over six extra hours were spent because of the different connotations of a single word—*interest*. When the Americans said that they wanted an interest in the Singapore business, they meant they wanted to buy into the company. When the Asians heard the word interest, they understood it to mean "interested" or "concerned," so they thought the Americans were saying they were concerned about the Singapore company. Hours later, as the misunderstanding was finally recognized and resolved, the negotiation went smoothly.

COMMUNICATION IS CULTURAL

Communication is influenced by cultural differences. Even the choice of medium to be used to communicate may be different for various countries. For example, it has been noted that advanced industrialized nations heavily use electronic communication technology and emphasize written communication over oral or face-to-face communication. Certainly the United States, Canada and Germany exemplify this trend. But Japan, which has access to the latest communications technologies, relies more on face-to-face oral communications than the written mode. The determining factor may not be the degree of industrialization, but rather whether the country falls into high context or low context cultures.

In his various books anthropologist Edward Hall makes a vital distinction between high and low context cultures, and how this matter of context impacts communication. In high context cultures, like that of Japan, much of the message is left unspecified—to be accessed through the context, nonverbal cues and between-the-lines interpretation of what is actually said. In contrast, in North American countries, which are low context cultures, messages are expected to be explicit and specific—and little is left for the receiver to deduce from the context.

Unless global managers are aware of subtle differences, it could lead to communication misunderstanding when Japanese and American managers attempt to work together, or when Latin and Northern Europeans seek to negotiate. The former are looking for meaning and understanding in what is *not* said—in the nonverbal communication or body language, in the silences and pauses, in relationships and empathy. The latter place emphasis on sending and receiving accurate messages directly, usually by being definite and articulate with spoken or written words.

YOU ARE WHAT YOU SPEAK

There is a joke that goes,

Q: "What do you call a person who can speak two languages?"

A: "Bilingual."

Q: "What do you call a person who can speak three languages?"

A: "Trilingual."

Q: "What do you call a person who can speak just one language?"

A: "An American."

We in Northern America have often been criticized by our international business partners and customers for our refusal to recognize that our clients, customers and business partners may not all speak English. In this regard we still have a long way to go. A management consulting firm conducted a survey of 256 United States international executives, of whom 75 percent were born in the U.S. and spent an average of 88 days on business outside North America. Almost 60 percent of respondents spent two to four months abroad each year. Twenty-five percent spent over four months. Sixty percent of these international executives had lived outside their country in the course of their business careers for a median of 3.3 years. Yet, only 44 percent expressed fluency in another language than English.

For many years American companies had been noted for using English as the only way to communicate with foreign clients and employees. Only recently, the chairmen of major U.S. corporations, from IBM to UPS, have directed their corporate communication, investor relations and international marketing managers to do what the Germans and Japanese have been doing all along— they are now producing employee newsletters, press releases, annual reports and sales brochures in a multitude of languages.

AT&T is one company that has turned the need for multiple language trans-lation into a market niche opportunity. AT&T Language Line allows customers to communicate with their non-English-speaking customers and business contacts by using interpreters on conference calls. From the Language Line communication center in Monterey, California, a network of interpreters is available in over 140 different languages. Some companies are taking this service to its next logical step and are reaching across oceans with mail order business and 24-hour-a-day customer service lines.

TWO CASES IN POINT

Lands' End Inc., the $700-million-a-year mail order company has relied on the Language Line for three years to keep in touch with the global community. The company, which estimates that it has 6.1 million customers worldwide, receives about 1,000 interna-tional calls per month and uses Language line for about 1 percent of those calls. Lands' End felt it couldn't serve foreign customers without a reliable translation service.

Gerber Products uses the Language Line to facilitate the company's 24-hour 800 number that invites questions on child care issues and receives inquiries from some 45,000 nervous mothers and fathers every month. Gerber products are sold around the globe, and the company receives several hundred calls a month from French-speaking and Spanish-speaking customers. In a recent month the company referred 360 French language calls and another 150 calls in Spanish to the Language Line.

Gerber is opening a plant in Poland and expects it will need interpretation services for those parents in Eastern Europe. Says Rita Van Boven, manager of consumer relations, "Gerber is a quality name, and we need to do these things to service our customers."

A consortium has been formed to develop and promote a lingua franca for the electronic age, a universal digital code that could be used by computers to represent letters and characters in all the world's languages. According to an article in the *Wall Street Journal*, the consortium consists of twelve members which are often fierce rivals, such as IBM, Apple Computer, Microsoft, Sun Microsystems and Xerox.

"If the code, called Unicode, becomes a worldwide standard, it would be easier for people in different countries to communicate by electronic mail," says Andrew Pollack, *New York Times* author. He adds that the code would also make it easier for software companies to develop programs that can work in different languages. "With the new code, any computer anywhere could understand and display everything from French accents to Chinese ideographs."

Metaphor Computer Systems, a software company in Mountain View, California, is serving as the headquarters of the Unicode, Inc., consortium. David Liddle, Metaphor's president, said, "The American computer software companies were able to put aside their differences to work on the standard because all of them see their overseas markets becoming more important."

INTERNATIONAL PRESENTATIONS

In today's growing global business environment, saying what you mean and meaning what you say are not always sufficient. You need to make sure that what you say translates into what you mean. *N'est-ce pas?*

There are many potential pitfalls for Americans presenting ideas to foreigners. A questionnaire on the subject of international communications was completed by 204 global business people from the United States. Fully 80 percent of the respondents reported difficulties conducting business with foreigners because of the latter's misunderstanding of American English.

Although English is becoming a global language, bear in mind that many people speak it as a second language and may have difficulty comprehending compared to those for whom it is a native language. Also note that American language is different from, although rooted in, British English, which is further modified as it is used in the British Commonwealth nations.

The problem lies with us. As a professional speaker to international audiences, I have learned the hard way—by embarrassing trial and error—that some "Americanisms" just don't readily translate across borders. While it is difficult to erase all American buzzwords, puns, gags, business jargon, sports metaphors and euphemisms from your speaking style, the consequence of not doing so is the risk of international misunderstanding.

Let's take a look at a few of the most common language offenses:

○ Humor

○ Slang

○ Jargon

○ Metaphor

○ Abbreviations

Humor

"Did you hear the one about the Scotsman who . . . ?" Well, if you did, keep it to yourself. While locals can poke fun at their government, highways, neighbors and themselves, don't you be tempted to join them. There are few things that an American might do that are more offensive than making a joke at the expense of his or her host country.

On the other hand, humor which is directed at yourself can have the positive effect of gaining audience empathy. And, while sometimes humor is definitely out of place, genuine warmth never is. One of the international executives I interviewed told me, "You can make a lot of communications mistakes, and people will overlook them, if they believe that you sincerely meant well."

Slang

"Run that by me again"

"Throwing the baby out with the bathwater"

"Go for it"

"It will never fly"

You and I may know exactly what these mean, but for much of the world's population, they are just confusing or meaningless expressions.

Jargon

"Buzzword"

"Dog and pony show"

"Walk your talk"

It may be colorful to us, but jargon is a barrier to clear communication and shows a lack of cultural sensitivity. Good intercultural communicators are also advised to be aware of all "American exuberances"—like calling things "fantastic" or "fabulous" (which, to a foreigner, may sound like you mean that things are "unreal" or "imaginary") or describing lunch as a "disaster" because the food was under-cooked (when foreigners use the word disaster to refer only to a real tragedy.)

Metaphor

"Monday morning quarterbacking"

"Waiting for the other shoe to fall"

"You struck out"

We in the United States are particularly fond of using sports metaphors in business presentations. It is easy to forget that almost all metaphors (including those referring to games played in the host country) are culturally appropriate and meaningful only where we learned them.

Abbreviations

R&D

CEO

P&L

Transnational communicators realize that using initials and abbreviations, which are basic English to us, are probably alphabet soup to everyone else.

"An American businessman had been negotiating a potential joint venture with a Japanese counterpart, but the discussion wasn't very productive. Then the American's potential partner offered a few key concessions. The American responded with relief, 'This makes it a whole new ballgame.' Unfortunately, because the interpreter translated this statement literally, the Japanese businessman believed the American doubted his seriousness and thought that he was just playing around. This incident was a serious setback to the process of trust building."

From *Hemispheres Magazine*, February 1993.

TRANSLATORS AND INTERPRETERS

In many business situations, international business people invariably face the problem of needing to communicate with foreign counterparts who do not speak their language. The solution, in most cases, is to use an interpreter.

Whenever I give a presentation to a non-English-speaking audience, I work with a professional interpreter. I provide him or her with a complete text of my speech beforehand. Once I have given the interpreter the written outline of my remarks, I do not stray from the script. (At a World Congress in Rome, the translators in several instances ignored ad lib comments from presenters who deviated from their texts because it was too hard to keep up with the pace).

Even if you're only using an interpreter in business meetings, it is best to give your interpreter the text (or at least an outline) of what you intend to say. In situations requiring specialized or technical vocabulary, also provide a glossary of terms. Just as the international speaker has to be sensitive to translation issues, the business person needs to understand the nuances of working with interpreters.

A CASE IN POINT

Former President Reagan tells a story about a speech he made in Mexico City. After his speech, he says, "I sat down to a rather unenthusiastic and not very impressive applause, and I was a little embarrassed. It was worse when a gentleman followed me and started speaking in Spanish, which I didn't understand, but he was being applauded about every paragraph. So, to hide my embarrassment, I started clapping before everyone else until our ambassador leaned over to me and said, 'I wouldn't do that if I were you. He's interpreting your speech.'"

When in doubt regarding the clarity of the message you are having translated, ask for a reverse interpretation. The head of corporate communications for an American organization that had just acquired a facility in France gave me this example: "I had written an entire speech for our president to give to the new French employees. I was assured that the translation was perfect. Just to be on the safe side, I asked for a reverse translation. It was a good thing that I did. One of the statements the CEO was to make was originally written as, 'Our products meet the basic needs of mankind.' The translated version was, 'Our products give the world an enema.'"

SEEING IS BELIEVING

In international business presentations the use of visual aids can help make sure that key points have been understood. In various circumstances, I've seen good results when verbal presentations are augmented with the use of charts, diagrams, photographs, outlines, models, displays and actual demonstrations.

Yet even in a visual format, you must be careful to understand and respond to differences in perception. For instance, when two people look at the same communication piece, each will come away with a different impression, but if the two are from different cultures, those impressions may vary enormously.

It is vitally important to understand international audiences and to adapt visual images to suit cultural backgrounds. For instance, you should avoid using triangular shapes in Hong Kong, Korea or Taiwan, as the triangle is considered a negative shape in those countries. And did you know that the number 7 is considered bad luck in Kenya, Ghana and Singapore, good luck in Czechoslovakia, and has magical connotations in Benin?

Certain images become powerful symbols in different cultures. The stork symbolizes maternal death (not birth) in Singapore, the owl is bad luck in India (like our black cat), and a green hat in China marks a man with an unfaithful wife. Some symbols are part of the national or religious pride and cannot be commercialized without running the risk of causing resentment. (Using a picture of Buddha, for example, is risky.)

The well-known anthropologist Edward T. Hall years ago noticed how casually Americans treat colors. We use colors situationally and decoratively. We may have our favorite colors or combinations, but the colors themselves have little or no significance. This is not the case in much of the rest of the world. In many cultures colors have great symbolic significance. Depending on the occasion, the color of clothing, gift wrapping or advertisements can cause great embarrassment and misunderstanding.

The color yellow, for instance, has religious and mystical overtones in India. In China it represents both the Emperor and pornography. In the United States it may evoke cowardice (yellow streak) or faithfulness (yellow ribbon). And if you wear yellow and green in Brazil, you'll be a laughing stock as those are the colors of the flag and no Brazilian wears them.

Black is not universal for mourning. In Brazil they wear purple, in Mexico they wear yellow, in many Asian countries mourners wear white, and in the Ivory Coast they wear dark red. Americans think of blue as the more masculine color, but in the United Kingdom or France, they favor red. Pink is feminine in the

U.S., while yellow is the favorite for most of the rest of the world. Red suggests good fortune in China, but death in Turkey.

GETTING YOUR MESSAGE ACROSS

Dealing in an international community, getting your message across correctly is increasingly important and difficult. To limit embarrassing and often costly mistakes, international communicators offer the following tips:

Know your substance and be well prepared.

Conform to basic grammar rules more strictly than is common in everyday conversation. Most English-speaking foreigners have a rudimentary knowledge of sentence structure and a limited vocabulary, but often their grammar is better than ours.

Practice using the most common 3,000 words in English. That is, those words typically learned in the first two years of language study.

When in a meeting, speak slowly and pronounce clearly. Paraphrase your response and recap your position often.

Pause after every three or four sentences, and plan your presentation so that each group of sentences conveys a single topic or unit.

Explain the major ideas two or three ways.

If you pause to ask your listeners if they understood, either do it lightly ("It's a complicated subject. Did I go too fast?") or put the onus on yourself ("Sometimes I speak too quickly. Shall I go over that again?").

Avoid uncommon or esoteric words. Use "effective" rather than "efficacious."

Avoid the use of negative wordings of a sentence when a positive form could be used.

Whenever possible, select an action-oriented verb (e.g., "ride the bus") rather than a general action verb (e.g., "take the bus").

Become aware of alternate spellings that exist of commonly used words and the regions in which those spellings are used: color/colour, organization/organisation, center/centre.

Stop periodically and ask, "Is that perfectly clear?" Don't wait until the end of the presentation before checking for comprehension.

Don't take yes for an answer. Ask probing questions that prove how much your listener is really absorbing.

Carefully monitor the listener's facial expression for signs of confusion. Look for glazed expressions and the wandering or sleepy eye that will tell you that you have lost your audience.

Be expressive and use gestures to support verbal messages.

In most cultures it is advisable always to maintain a pleasant disposition and not show signs of anger.

During meetings write out the main points that were discussed.

After meetings confirm in writing what has been agreed.

If you are using an interpreter, in addition to the above list, you should also be aware of the following advice:

Remember to speak to the person with whom you are dealing and not to the interpreter. If culturally appropriate, maintain eye contact and convey interest.

Permit the interpreter to spend as much time as needed in clarifying points whose meanings are obscure.

Do not interrupt the interpreter as he or she translates, as interrupting causes many misunderstandings.

Do not work an interpreter over two or three hours without allowing time for him or her to rest. If a lengthy negotiation period is anticipated, you might even use two different interpreters.

Both parties in a negotiation should employ their own interpreters. This avoids overload on one person and also avoids the possibility that the interpreter will unconsciously represent best the interest of his or her employer.

It may be that an interpreter is skilled in linguistics and still not familiar with the nuances of business or negotiation. If so, you can hire a bicultural adviser who serves as a cultural broker on how best to prepare yourself and your presentation.

Take responsibility for all misunderstandings and mistakes.

Practice using an interpreter before the situation requires you to do so. At the very least, if you have a bilingual colleague, ask him or her to review your text and visual presentation.

MISCOMMUNICATIONS

Global communication and miscommunication have always had a humorous side. The European Economic Community collected some of the worst abuses of the Queen's English from around the world. Under the title "Mind Your Language," these fractured phrases were displayed on boards in the lobbies of the EEC's Centre Borschette office complex in Belgium.

Take the Paris hotel that told guests: "Please leave your values at the desk." Or the Bangkok dry cleaner's request: "Drop your trousers here for best results." And what did an Austrian ski resort mean when it urged guests "not to preambulate the corridors in the hours of repose in the boots of ascension?"

A few other examples from this list of linguistic mishaps:

An Acapulco hotel reassured guests about the drinking water: "The manager has personally passed all water served here."

A Tokyo hotel advised guests: "It is forbidden to steal towels please. If you are not a person to do such things, please not to read notice."

Another Tokyo hotel, seemingly more relaxed about morals, said: "You are invited to take advantage of the chambermaid."

A notice in a Norwegian cocktail lounge stated: "Ladies are requested not to have children in the bar."

A Prague tourist agency urged tourists to: "Take one of our horse-driven city tours. We guarantee no miscarriages."

In the Copenhagen airport, one airline promised to: "Take your bags and send them in all directions."

When these language miscommunications happen to other people, they are indeed humorous. When they happen to us, they are not always so funny! It is because of examples like the ones listed below that more international companies now rely on country-specific public relations and advertising firms to handle their global publicity and promotion:

○ The Sunbeam Corporation wanted to advertise a new mist-producing hair curling iron called "The Mist Stick" in Germany without realizing that in German the word *mist* means "dung" or "manure." Luckily, the problem was spotted right before the advertising campaign began.

○ When Kentucky Fried Chicken put up billboards to announce that their product was "finger lickin' good," the slogan was translated into Chinese as a rather unappetizing "bite your fingers off."

○ When General Motors introduced its Chevy Nova model to Spanish-speaking markets, it was without taking into account that in Spanish, Nova (*no va*) means "no go." Given this, it's no surprise that the Nova was a big disappointment in Spanish-speaking markets. No one, after all, wanted to buy a car that, by its very name, indicated it didn't work.

○ An often-cited example of miscommunication is Coca-Cola's advertising when that soda was first introduced into the Asian market. The firm's name and product were translated into Chinese characters that sounded correct, but actually read, "Bite the wax tadpole." Not to be outdone, Pepsi-Cola had a comparable communication disaster when it moved into the Thai market using their American slogan, "Come alive, you're in the Pepsi generation." Only later did their managers discover that the real Thai translation said, "Pepsi brings your ancestors back from the dead."

○ Images can have highly symbolic meaning in different cultures. A recent television commercial created quite a controversy in its Hong Kong audiences. The feminine hygiene product featured a "voice-over" while the screen showed flower pedals floating gently to the ground. The company obviously didn't realize that falling petals are a Chinese symbol for losing one's virginity.

However, not all miscommunications are even mildly amusing. In fact, some misinterpretations have had tragic results. This example is from the book *How We Discommunicate*, by public relations practitioner Philip Lesly:

> "A Japanese word, mokusatsu, may have changed all our lives. It has two meanings: (1) to ignore, (2) to refrain from comment. The release of a press statement using the second meaning in July, 1945, might have ended the war (World War II) then. The Emperor was ready to end it, and had the power to do so. The cabinet was ready to accede to the Potsdam ultimatum of the Allies—surrender or be crushed—but wanted a little more time to discuss the terms. A press release was prepared announcing the policy mokusatsu, with the no comment interpretation. But if on the foreign wires with the ignores interpretation through a mix-up in translation: 'The cabinet ignores the demand to surrender.'
>
> To recall the release would have entailed an unthinkable loss of face. Had the intended meaning been publicized, the cabinet might have backed up the Emperor's decision to surrender. In which event, there might have been no atomic bombs over Hiroshima and Nagasaki. Tens of thousands of Japanese might have been saved. One word, misinterpreted."

CHAPTER

7

The International Assignment

“Ninety-nine point nine percent of all expatriate failures happen because of cultural adjustment problems. In a sense, it's similar to why people fail on the job in this country. People aren't fired because they lack technical competence: they're fired because they can't get along.”

—Ken Yeager, President
Commodities International

“Probably between $2 billion and $2.5 billion a year is lost from failed foreign transfers.”

—J. Stewart Black, Associate Professor
Dartmouth's Tuck School

GOING ABROAD

Several years ago, a friend of mine accompanied her husband, an executive for an international legal firm, on a two-year business assignment to Saudi Arabia. The couple, who made the move with their three teenagers, were given no cross-cultural training prior to departure, no assistance once they arrived in the Middle East and no counseling to prepare them for repatriation once the assignment was over. All questions about their new home—from how to socialize on the job to where to buy a light bulb—went unanswered.

My friends met the challenge of relocation in spite of the lack of preparation, but many people in similar circumstances do not. Some ill-prepared expatriates are early returns, and others stay the length of their contracts but are marginal performers.

While some amount of cultural insight is applicable to all relocation experiences, whether domestic or international, anticipating the unique challenges of another culture becomes paramount for success in foreign assignments. As a result of their inability to cope with bewildering cultural differences, many families return to U.S. soil within a few months of deployment, costing their organizations valuable time, money and opportunities. Here are a couple of examples from my interviews:

> *"Just getting the 'basics' for existence was much more difficult than I thought it would be. We weren't prepared. For one thing, I didn't realize that apartments would be so bare—without carpets, drapes, flooring or even electrical outlets. There were three lovely bathrooms, but no running water. And God knows how long we would have had to wait to get a telephone installed."*

> *"We couldn't make it work for us. I was on the road a lot, and all my energy was going into learning the new job. The kids were in school. But my wife was totally on her own. She couldn't get a work permit, and so she felt isolated, bored and lonely. Even though I liked the work, it wasn't worth the strain on our marriage."*

Without a system of selection and cross-cultural preparation, an organization faces costly penalties. Premature return of an employee and family sent on an overseas assignment may cost the company upwards of $200,000, depending on the employee's salary, the location, and the size of the family to be transferred. And while the direct costs may be quite high, the damage goes beyond that cost. An assignment failure can diminish the company's worldwide reputation, leading to ramifications beyond those of the particular affiliate. A failure affects the morale of all employees in the two parts of the organization and interferes with the relationship between the two entities. Most destructively of all, it inhibits the organization's growth by preventing the company from seizing opportunities.

In this important chapter we will look at international assignments from four different angles:

○ The reasons why organizations relocate personnel internationally.

○ The advantages of international relocation for the employee.

○ The potential pitfalls of relocation.

○ Organizational strategies for assuring successful overseas assignments.

CORPORATE ADVANTAGES TO FOREIGN ASSIGNMENTS

Building a world-class organization begins with developing world-class talent. If you want your company to be global, you need managers who are ready and able to tackle global issues. Companies that compete in the global marketplace are finding that they need to develop an in-house pool of managers with international experience and perspective. Strategically orchestrating cross-national assignments provides firms with an opportunity to grow this talent.

The movement of employees around different parts of the organization based in different countries creates cross-fertilization and a truly global perspective. International relocation can develop and strengthen the skills, sensitivities and viewpoints of individuals, which in turn leads to enhanced contribution from those individuals. (Dow Chemical is just one example of an organization that uses worldwide job rotations to make employees comfortable globally.) It is through such transfers that firms develop international experience and viewpoint, providing another opportunity for the learning organization to improve itself.

Sometimes employee relocation is a product of international recruitment. Unilever has had a worldwide recruiting effort since the 1930s. They believe that to get the best candidates, the company must initially draw from a worldwide pool.

Often, it is the unique business needs of an organization that makes global relocation desirable. Foreign assignments can be the result of the need to transfer technology, transfer product or transfer knowledge. An example of technology would be a semiconductor manufacturing process; an example of a product would be a customer engineering technical operations group that is assisting in the announcement phase of products; and the transfer of knowledge might be an individual who has special knowledge of European compensation programs and is assigned to corporate staff to help create a global compensation package.

EMPLOYEE ADVANTAGES TO INTERNATIONAL RELOCATION

People who relish international assignments do so for a variety of reasons: some like the adventure of living in foreign places, some simply have wanderlust and like to travel as much as possible, and some look forward to the learning experience that comes with becoming saturated by a new people, culture and language. An executive for a chemical company told me, "My wife and I have relocated all over the world. We've loved every minute of it. What an incredible opportunity to travel and meet people and to learn about different cultures. It has been a lifetime of ongoing education. We wouldn't have missed it for any-thing!" But the most common reason that people accept overseas assignments is that they love the professional challenge and inherent rewards. In fact, many expatriates I interviewed have absolutely no interest in returning to the United States. In the words of one Asian manager, "Here I am pretty autonomous. My responsibil-ities are tremendous, and my territory covers six countries. After all this, how could I ever be content back at the home office in Cincinnati?"

In today's global market many executives are trying to make sure that they are viewed as cosmopolitan. A person may use international assignments to develop expertise in multiple functions and locations.

David Johnson, the chief executive officer of Campbell soup, began his career as a management trainee with Colgate-Palmolive International in Australia. He moved through marketing and management positions to become chairman and managing director of Colgate's South African operations in 1967. In 1973 he moved to Hong Kong as president of Warner-Lambert/Parke-Davis Asia. That company brought him to the United States in 1976 as president of its Personal Products Division. When Warner-Lambert acquired Entenmann's in 1979, Mr. Johnson took over as its head. Next came Gerber Products in 1987 and then the top executive position at Campbell Soup.

As he reported in a recent interview, if there was ever a turning point for Mr. Johnson—more like an awakening to an even higher level of enthusiasm—it came when he transferred to Hong Kong at age 40. There he marveled at the Orient's fundamentally different practices, approaches, customs and traditions. He learned that there were infinite solutions to business problems. All you needed was the creativity to look beyond the accepted ones. "I had an elasti-cized mind, opened to a greater run of possibilities than I'd ever known before."

POTENTIAL PITFALLS TO RELOCATION

A few years ago, I was hired by Allied Van Lines to do a study on the "human side" of relocation—why people decide to take relocation offers and why they may decline. Since that time I have expanded my interviews to focus on the trials and successes of overseas relocations. One of the first things I noticed was the increasing difficulty companies are having in attracting qualified home-country nationals to accept foreign assignments. United States and European companies cite some common problems with respect to persuading promising executives to accept international relocations:

○ Foreign positions are no longer viewed as glamorous as they used to be. Executives and their families value a comfortable and familiar life-style more.

○ Employees have multiple loyalties—commitment to the organization may be competing with family considerations and other "quality of life" issues. People are less likely to make moves that are seen as personal sacrifices for an organization.

○ Ambitious and qualified managers are concerned about what will happen to their careers after they return from overseas. They are afraid (and often rightly so) that they will return from an international assignment and find little appreciation for their accomplishments back home. Often, the move abroad is perceived as "banishment."

○ The schooling of children and the care of elder dependents are two crucial considerations. If satisfactory arrangements cannot be made with regard to these issues, otherwise satisfactory relocations may be declined.

○ The diversity of today's family makes relocation more difficult. In the past, male executives would pack up their homemaker wives and 2.3 children—and off they'd go. Today's relocating managers may be male or female. They may be single parents, live with stepchildren, have noncustodial offspring or have joint custody of their children.

○ Managers want international assignments to be limited to a specific number of years. While in the past, organizations could get a commitment to stay overseas until a particular project was completed, today people want a finite arrangement.

○ Dual-career couples are becoming a barrier to getting an individual to accept a foreign post. Relocations are more often being evaluated by two people whose combined income and career advancement opportunities must be taken into consideration.

SUCCESSFUL ORGANIZATIONAL STRATEGIES AND POLICIES

All of these problems make a foreign assignment boil down to a focal point. The individual has become more important in the corporate scheme of things than was previously the case, and companies are having to develop policies to accommodate the needs and concerns of affected people.

International employees go through a predictable series of stages transferring from a domestic to an international assignment and back home again. The keys to successful international relocations include viable corporate objectives for the assignment and appropriate selection of assignees and families, followed by thorough preparation of the individual and family members, active support while on assignment, and then a well-planned reentry and career strategy.

Viable corporate objectives provide the foundation for overseas activities. A thoughtful selection process sets the stage for tailoring a program to integrate the person into the position and the culture, and to counsel the family in its adjustment. Based on the information gained in this process, a detailed support system can be set in place, followed by a personalized preparation for repatriation and career progression.

Step #1: Corporate Objectives

To ensure expatriate effectiveness and to maximize their investment in overseas personnel, companies need innovative international HR approaches which begin with a comprehensive, culturally appropriate corporate plan for international activities.

Upper management sometimes isn't aware of the impact of culture on global business operations and expatriate performance. Interviews with foreign nationals, managers who have had overseas experience from their own and other companies, and on-site expatriates can help the organization develop expertise on the successful behaviors and ways of doing business in various countries. With this information an international plan can be developed which establishes clear, realistic international objectives with bicultural strategies for implementation.

To meet their overall worldwide goals, corporate approaches must recognize, integrate and optimize cultural differences. To overlook such important factors will almost always lead to less than optimal results.

A U.S. telecommunications firm contracted to transfer a certain technology to a local firm in Saudi Arabia. The performance deadlines for the Saudi trainees were impossible to meet, given the trainees' lack of educational background, usual work hours and limited language competency. The frustrated American expatriates ended up doing the trainees' work for them to meet the deadlines and never achieved their main objective of transferring the technology.

Step #2: The Selection

Many organizations focus on finding individuals with functional skills needed for international work and overlook the importance of cultural savvy. Of course the company and the candidate both need to be aware of the actual job responsibilities of the position in the affiliate organization, and the expectations of how the position will function should be clearly spelled out. But most expatriate failures are not caused by problems with job skills. They're caused by the inability of the employee (or the employee's family) to cope with and adapt to an unfamiliar culture.

Culture sets the ground rules for business communications and management behavior. Culture defines the challenges and opportunities of social interaction and daily life. When international personnel-selection decisions are made primarily on the basis of a person's professional accomplishments and availability, it addresses only some of the needed qualifications. Because of the unique adaptation demands of such assignments, success in the position is not guaranteed by professional credentials, expertise or availability. Personal characteristics and family circumstances weigh heavily in the issue of how well employees will adapt to the demands of the new culture.

Between 20 percent and 50 percent of the personnel sent abroad return prematurely from their cross-national assignments. According to the Business Council for International Understanding, the expatriate failure rate is as follows: 18 percent in London, 27 percent in Brussels, 36 percent in Tokyo; and in Saudi Arabia, 68 out of every 100 Americans will come home early because of their inability to cross the cultural chasm.

The key is to select employees who, in addition to technical skills, possess the characteristics and attitudes required for intercultural effectiveness. There are variants of effective management and effective managerial characteristics, based as much on cultural as corporate expectations. Productive cross-national assignments rest on the fit between position, culture and person.

There is no stereotypical mold, no single set of personality factors which will guarantee that some international managers will succeed and others will fail. There is, however, a general sense of which characteristics are most likely to show up in successful expatriates. I interviewed executives who had lived and managed abroad for several years to give me their opinions of the factors necessary for success in international assignments. Here are their qualifications:

Supportive Family

"The key to a successful relocation is strong family support. This is an expatriate team *going overseas. If the family suffers too much, the burden and guilt felt by the employee is a massive energy drain."*

"First of all, you need a spouse with a high degree of creativity and resourcefulness."

Interpersonal Skills

"You need to be able to manage people extremely well. You will need all of the interpersonal and management skills that you used in the United States, and then some."

"Because of their human relations savvy, we are finding that female managers are very successful culturally with international assignments."

Confidence

"If you are not confident—I don't care what else you are—you won't make it on the international management scene. And you've got to learn to show personal strength and confidence in understated ways. You've got to react to uncomfortable situations with little outward sign of irritation. You can't go around shouting and banging on desks."

"If you want to create a generalist, send a manager overseas. He will have more responsibility—and find himself handling more pieces of the business—than he ever dreamed. He'd better be confident."

Flexibility

"The key to success in overseas assignments is flexibility. It doesn't matter how you did it back home, I can assure you that you'll be doing it differently over here. So you can't be threatened by those differences."

"If you keep an open mind, you'll discover that there are many ways to get the job done."

Cultural Sensitivity

"Many Western managers are so concerned with getting the job done that they only focus on the task side of the job. When you are transferring information and skills to persons in another culture, how you do it is at least as important as what you do."

"You've got to counteract the tendency to make quick, simplistic assessments of situations. These are complex societies, comprised of different ethnic or religious groups, various class or caste stratas, with regional and geographic barriers and rural and urban populations. So you can't afford to make pat generalizations or quick assumptions."

Cultural Respect

"The thing to be kept uppermost in mind is that you are a guest in your assigned country. There is nothing more appalling to me than to see the 'ugly American expatriate' who openly ridicules the host

*country and compares everything to 'the much better way we do it' in
the U.S."*

*"You've got to go into the new country respecting and trusting people . . .
at least until they prove unworthy of that trust and respect. You might
get disappointed sometimes, but if you can't go in with that up-front
attitude, you will accomplish very little with the locals."*

Step #3: Preparing for Relocation

Initially, the candidate and family must have adequate, accurate infor-mation
about the assignment and location for them to make an informed decision.
Both the employee and spouse should be well briefed on the actual job
responsibilities. (What will this person really be doing in the affiliate organization? How will the position function in relation to both the affiliate and the
home office? What will the work-related entertainment responsibilities be?)
Other important issues need to be addressed: What are the company's expatriate policies regarding compensation, benefits, physical relocation arrangements, security procedures and repatriation? All of this information should be
given accurately and thoroughly before departure so that people have an
unromanticized view of their assignment.

In her excellent textbook *International Dimensions of Organizational Behavior*,
author Nancy J. Adler describes the process of cross-cultural adjustment to a
foreign country as a U-shaped curve. At the beginning of the foreign assignment, anticipation and excitement are high. (Business travelers, as compared to
expatriates, often have the luxury of remaining in this state.) This has been
referred to as the stage of euphoria.

When the excitement starts to wane, people become disillusioned. No matter
what they thought the foreign country would be like, there are the inevitable
disappointments and frustrations—the language is more difficult to master than
they thought it would be, some of the behaviors (in business and in daily life)
that worked successfully back home are totally inappropriate in the new culture.
At this stage people can become frustrated and irritable as they focus on the
differences and difficulties of the new culture.

The bottom of the curve has been labeled "culture shock"—the confusion and
depression that can come from the constant bombardment of things they don't
understand and behaviors that don't make sense. At this point people either

give up and go back home, or they learn to adapt and acclimate to the new culture—to accept some cultural frustrations along with the high points.

If they can adapt to the new culture, expatriates generally begin to feel more positive, work more effectively, and have a more normal life. Full recovery results in an ability to function in two cultures with comfort and confidence.

Professor W. J. Redden developed a *Culture Shock Inventory* to identify those individuals who are more prone to suffer from this malady. His premise is that "culture shock is a psychological disorientation caused by misunderstanding or not understanding the cues from another culture. It arises from such things as lack of knowledge, limited prior experience, and personal 'rigidity.' "

Therefore, he assesses persons going on foreign deployment on eight measures. These categories are interesting as they provide clues to be cultivated in order to successfully cope in the international arena. The eight measures are:

1. **Western Ethnocentrism**—the degree to which the Western value system is seen as appropriate for other parts of the world.

2. **Intercultural Experience**—the degree of direct experience with people from other countries, through working, traveling and conversing; also learned skills, such as language and culture studies.

3. **Cognitive Flex**—the degree of openness to new ideas, beliefs and experience, and the ability of the individual to accept these.

4. **Behavioral Flex**—the degree to which one's own behavior is open to change or alteration; the ability to experiment with new styles.

5. **Cultural Knowledge: Specific**—the degree of awareness and understanding of various customs, beliefs and patterns of behavior in a specific other culture.

6. **Cultural Knowledge: General**—the degree of awareness, sensitivity and understanding of various beliefs and institutions in other cultures.

7. **Cultural Behavior**—the degree of awareness and understanding of patterns of cultural differences and human behavior.

8. **Interpersonal Sensitivity**—the degree of awareness and understanding of verbal and nonverbal human behavior.

The role of cross-cultural preparation is *not* to try to obliterate culture shock, but rather to help people anticipate and accept it as a healthy part of the culturation process, and to find ways to lessen its stressful impact. Some organizations offer relocation programs "inhouse" while others contract with "third-party" providers who specialize in international moves. In either case much confusion and potential cost can be saved by adequate information and counseling up front.

The goal is to provide training and orientation for the employee and family members that will equip them with the information, skills and attitudes necessary to be comfortable, effective and productive overseas. A full range of programs is needed for preparation of the employee and his/her family.

For the employee:

○ Definitive guidelines and job performance expectations, including the length of the international assignment.

○ Career counseling in regards to career progression and job assignment upon repatriation.

○ Cross-cultural communication and management training.

○ Intercultural business and negotiation skills.

For the employee and spouse:

○ Language training. (For maximum benefit this can be sequenced pre-departure and in-country.)

○ Culture shock management.

○ Stress control training.

○ Children's education planning.

○ Spouses trained to understand the stresses and challenges that their husbands or wives will face on the job, and transferring employees taught to understand the stresses and responsibilities that spouses face.

○ Host country daily living issues and life-style adjustment.

○ Local customs and etiquette.

○ Pre-assignment trip to the country of destination to look at housing and get a feel for the people and their customs.

○ Continued cross-cultural indoctrination by lectures, films, books, cassettes, videos, etc.

For the entire family:

○ Spousal counseling in career challenges and opportunities.

○ Children's counseling sessions.

Nearly half of major U.S. companies now give executives cross-cultural training before foreign transfers, compared to about 10 percent a decade ago. Is all this training and employee preparation worth the time and money it costs? Many organizations think so:

Jody Aurawski, manager of foreign service employees programs at S. C. Johnson, coordinates all cross-cultural training for the company's international work force of 13,000 employees spread across nineteen countries. She believes that training is well worth the investment. "Even if you spend $3,000 to train a person who decides after the training that he doesn't want to go," she says, "you've still saved at least $300,000—the combined cost of wages, taxes, rent, moving and other expenses—by finding that out ahead of time." The expatriate failure rate at Johnson Wax is less than 2 percent, an achievement Aurawsi attributes to cross-cultural training.

"American businesses are dumb if they don't use cross-cultural training," says Richard B. Jackson, personnel vice president of Reynolds Metal Company's overseas arm. The big aluminum maker's high rate of expatriate burnout fell "to almost zero," Mr. Jackson notes, after the company began using cross-cultural training in the late 1970s.

Despite massive cost cutting at General Motors, the auto giant still spends nearly $500,000 a year on cross-cultural training for about 150 Americans and their families headed abroad. "We think this substantially contributes to the low premature return rate of less than 1 percent among GM expatriates," says Richard Rachner, GM general director of international personnel.

Without an intensive preparation which includes cross-cultural training and which emphasizes the personal adjustments required for the move, employees and their families can feel resentful toward the organization. Too often that resentment results in less-than-optimal work productivity or in an early return home.

> *"I wish the company had prepared me for the differences in culture. It took me months of being totally out of sync before I finally caught on to what was required to get the job done. Until then, I was absolutely unproductive."*

> *"All I was told was the 'good stuff.' I feel like I've been 'set-up' by the company . . . like they didn't trust me with the whole truth. It's not a good feeling."*

Step #4: Cross-Cultural Entry

Culture shock is the expatriate's reaction to a new, unpredictable, and therefore uncertain environment. It's an understandable response to finding out that successful behaviors and attitudes back home will not get the same results in the new country. To help people adjust as soon as possible, international organizations provide services that serve as "culture shock absorbers." They offer assistance in locating housing, shopping, schools for children, social activities, banking, medical care, recreation facilities, and jobs for spouses. And then they follow up with ongoing support if needed. One executive explained it this way:

> *"The company has to coddle new expatriates so that employees believe that whatever problems they may encounter, the organization has encountered them and solved them before."*

Some organizations do a fine job in offering ongoing guidance and support to their international employees. Others are behind the times when it comes to responding to the needs of their expatriates. But no matter how well the company may assist its relocated employees, everyone must find for him or herself a personally satisfying way to handle the stress that comes with adjusting to the overseas work and daily life situations. The expatriates that I interviewed had a variety of stress-management approaches:

> *"Wherever I go, no matter how long the assignment is, I approach the new territory as if this is going to be my home from now on. For*

some reason I find that this attitude helps me adjust to a foreign country with the least amount of stress."

"I get totally immersed in the foreign culture. I learn the language, attend community functions and experiment with local food. Then, for balance, periodically I do things that are only related to the United States—like attending meetings at the American Chamber of Commerce or socializing at the American Club."

"I find that physical stamina is closely related to how much of a toll stress takes on me. If I'm eating correctly, resting enough and staying on my exercise program, I handle things a lot better."

"I have really learned the value of setting priorities since I relocated. It's a total waste of energy to 'sweat the little things.' You've got to let go of the things you can't control and focus on the most important tasks."

"My best advice for expatriates is to learn the language as soon as possible. It is amazing how much better you feel when you can understand and make yourself understood in day-to-day conversations."

"I keep a daily journal in which I record my frustrations and my successes. It helps me keep things in perspective."

Cultural adjustment is a process. Employees and their families may benefit from further training and support once they arrive overseas and begin to wrestle with the new realities. It also takes time before an expatriate adapts well enough to become a truly productive part of the regional work force. While various textbooks say that it takes three to six months to emerge from culture shock, many international executives tell me that new employees are "totally useless" for at least the first year. This is one of the reasons that short overseas assignments (the typical three-year term) are not considered a good policy by many senior managers abroad: "The first year people are getting adjusted, the second year they're finally doing the job, and the third year all they can think about is getting back home."

A family's poor adjustment causes more foreign-transfer failures than a manager's work performance. It certainly takes time for the spouse to adjust to dealing with the "raw cultural" issues of buying groceries, negotiating with vendors, getting children enrolled in school, communicating with neighbors and decoding the public transportation system. Furthermore, because most job transfers involve working couples, finding meaningful opportunities for an expatriate's spouse—the wife in 90 percent of all cases—is another challenge she faces.

A CASE IN POINT

On the occasions when the "trailing spouse" is male, the work situation doesn't always become easier. A female executive with an international hotel chain was transferred to Hong Kong. Her husband embraced the move as an opportunity to open his own training and consulting firm, only to find out that without an employer of record (his wife could not sponsor him), he was not allowed to work. After fruitless discussion with Hong Kong authorities, the husband gave up his idea of independence and applied for a position with an established firm.

Most repatriates report that coming home is far more difficult than leaving. Employees come back changed in some ways by the overseas experience. They return to an organization (and a country) that has changed as well. Their friends have moved, their children are out of touch with the latest slang or fashion, and the work skills they have honed overseas are not always respected by bosses back home.

Reentry issues for the employee's family encompass the same areas they faced before departure: the spouse's career, children's educational needs, housing, community reorientation, and so on. In effect, the family is dealing with reentry shock. Once again, the employee and his or her family can benefit from counseling and support.

> *"I had my children in the best schools abroad, and my house work and cooking taken care of by a maid. I forgot how hard it is to do everything myself."*

> *"In Hong Kong a woman alone can walk to the (711) alone at night and not be concerned for her safety. Has the United States always been this violent and I just never noticed before?"*

To some extent, one's very success in adjusting to the foreign culture becomes a stumbling block initially at home. The difficulty in readjusting to America can materialize in expectations large and small.

"In Japan the taxis all have automatic doors that the driver opens for the passenger. I can't tell you how stupid I felt in New York while I stood there waiting for the taxi door to open."

"When did the smog (traffic, overpopulation, school system, personal rudeness, etc.) get this bad in the United States?"

"We were astonished with the amount of red tape that we had to go through in the U.S. When we encountered this kind of obstruction while we lived in Europe, we'd say, 'We'd never have to put up with this at home!' "

Twenty percent of the employees who complete overseas assignments want to leave their firm when they come home. According to the *Wall Street Journal's* report of a survey of 34 multinational companies, "Bosses might quickly become sensitive if they added up the cost to the company."

Many employees return to organizations (or bosses) which do not value international business experience as critical to overall corporate success.

"I found out the meaning of 'out of sight, out of mind.' No one cares about what I learned overseas."

"No one wants to hear my story. They are so caught up in the way we operate in the United States, they don't see the value in thinking about things in any other context."

Many employees complain that their reentry jobs bore them. Almost half of the repatriated employees surveyed by Korn/Ferry International found their reentry positions less satisfying than their overseas positions.

"I'm just not challenged or excited by the work assignment my company gave me upon return to the U.S. The job doesn't give me the responsibility or authority I'm used to."

A plan for reentry should be in place before the person leaves for the assignment. Too often, reentering executives find themselves in career dilemmas brought on by lack of planning, inadequate career information and outdated promises from bosses—who may no longer be in their positions—as to what their roles in the company will be upon return. Prior to completion of the assignment, the organization should work with the employee to determine what position best fits the person's acquired skills as well as meeting his or her professional and personal goals.

For the organization, returning employees can be a powerful source of information. The valuable international skills and knowledge of personnel on foreign assignment should be reintegrated into the corporation throughout their time abroad and upon repatriation. Debriefing and reentry training sessions can facilitate the transition into the home organization as well as add significantly to the company's global knowledge. The employee needs to know how he or she might best be utilized in the company's strategy for success, and the home office personnel needs the feedback to better understand worldwide operations.

SUCCESSFUL ASSIGNMENTS STRENGTHEN THE ORGANIZATION

The explicit goals for a successful cross-national assignment are to choose the best person for the situation, optimize his or her effectiveness through adequate training and support, and in doing so, maximize the performance for the cross-national affiliate and the entire organization.

Retraining employees with international experience and talent will become more and more crucial to building companies that can compete effectively in the global marketplace. Probably the best thing that an organization can do to increase the success rate of its expatriates is to strengthen company support for the worth of international careers.

One very satisfied expatriate said of his company: "What you need are models of success like we have at our organization. Our chief executive officer was once the head of European operations. I have no doubt that this company values overseas experience."

IN SUMMARY

The world of organizations is no longer limited by national boundaries. The era of globalization is at hand. Globalization impacts the business practices of executives of international conglomerates as well as managers and workers within multinational organizations and entrepreneurs with small import/export operations.

With the globalization of knowledge, economies and markets, today's managers face their greatest challenges and opportunities. To prosper in this global marketplace, we all must learn to adjust to new ways of thinking and new ways of doing business. We must develop personal, organizational and national strategies that accept and anticipate the challenges of globalization while optimizing the inherent opportunities. *Managing in a Global Organization* was written to encourage all business people to "think globally," and to understand why we need to think in terms of new keys for success in a changing world.

In the first chapter we looked at globalization, not just as an interesting management theory, but as a matter of survival. The forces advancing globalization—changes in world economies, technological advances, power shifts and international competition—are accelerating. The first key to success in a changing world is to acknowledge the effect that globalization has on us and to expand our view of American businesses (of all sizes) to include the reality of multinational consumers, workers, facilities, resources, ideas and trends.

In the second chapter we discussed the changing structure of global organizations, and found another key to success—pushed by global forces, our competitive organizations will transform in ways that promote increased flexibility, shared values, a global vision for the future, "boundarylessness," a multinational perspective and employee empowerment.

The third chapter focused on necessary global management skills. The key to management success is to develop new behaviors and new attitudes that reflect a truly global perspective. Personal flexibility, excellent communication skills and a balance of logical and creative thinking processes are all part of today's management requirements, as are the abilities to explain and embody a global "mindset," to value and utilize diversity, to build local and global teams and to lead others—rather than just manage them.

No one can approach the subject of globalization without encountering the word CHANGE. The fourth chapter stated that global change is a way of life currently and for the foreseeable future. Our organizations are increasingly going to be operating in a state of transformation. Therefore, the fourth key to success is to understand, embrace and manage the change process in yourself and within your organization.

The fifth chapter talked about doing business internationally. With the expansion of multinational customers, suppliers and work force, cross-cultural competence becomes essential. The fifth key to success is to identify, understand and respect cultural differences.

Chapter six covered global communication—its challenges and its importance. Since there is no communication until the receiver has perceived and retained the message, cultural influences play a major role in the process. Nonverbal communication, vocabulary and phrasing, even colors and symbols can carry cultural charges that may obscure or enhance the message you want to deliver. The sixth key to success in a changing world is to communicate with the appropriate cultural awareness and sensitivity.

The international assignment was the topic of chapter seven. In it we looked at the advantages of international assignments for both employees and their organizations, and we discussed the potential pitfalls. The seventh key to success is to encourage and acknowledge the importance of international experience. For the organization that wants to be global, you need managers with global backgrounds who can tackle global issues. For the employee who wants to develop as a world-class talent, you can use international experience to increase your value to world-class organizations.

There is one additional section to this book. To be effective as a global manager and to stay current on developments within the global marketplace, you need to have ready access to reliable sources of global business information. It is to fill this need that I wrote the next section of the book. Chapter eight is the result of several months of research efforts, during which I compiled substantial lists of government agencies, reference books, directories, videos, pamphlets, international business organizations, educational programs and other resources which I felt would be helpful to anyone interested in international business. I offer this section of the book next, with the hope that it will serve as the basis and the inspiration for developing your own global library of refer-ences and resources—our final key to success in a changing world.

CHAPTER

8

Global Management Resources

The information contained in this chapter is a collection of resources that took me months to compile. There is no way that a list of references and resources is ever "finished." In this regard, all corrections, improvements or additions are encouraged and welcomed. Please send them to:

Carol Kinsey Goman, Ph.D.
Kinsey Consulting Services
P.O. Box 8255
Berkeley, CA 94707
Phone: 510-943-7850
Fax: 510-524-9577

SECTION A—BOOKS

The Age of Unreason
By Charles Handy. Publisher 1991.

In Brief:

In this fascinating book Charles Handy (visiting professor at the London Business School and consultant) shows how dramatic changes are transforming business, education and the nature of work. We can see them in astounding new developments in technology, in the shift in demand from manual to cerebral skills and in the virtual disappearance of lifelong, full-time jobs.

The author further contends that continuous change, however uncomfortable, is the only way forward, but to benefit from the changes, we need new kinds of organizations, new approaches to work, new types of schools and new ideas about the nature of our society.

Beyond Free Trade
Edited by David B. Yoffie. Harvard Business School Press, 1993.

In Brief:

This book grew from the convictions of David Yoffie and his colleagues that current debates about world trade are missing the depth and complexity of the tremendous changes taking place in the world economy. In looking at firms that actually move goods, services and capital around the world, the authors incorporate research on industries that cut across all spectrums: high tech, low tech, services, manufacturing and raw materials. They look at the ways in which politicians and firms now have the opportunity to restructure global competition.

Competition in Global Industries
Edited by Michael E. Porter. Harvard Business School Press, 1986.

In Brief:

This book provides a framework for understanding the nature of international competition in industries and its strategic implications for firms. It documents the historical transformation of international competition and shows how global competition changes the way marketing, production, government relations and finance should be managed. In-depth case studies illustrate the interplay of these factors in industries chosen to illuminate the issues facing today's managers.

Do's and Taboos Around the World
Edited by Roger E. Axtell. John Wiley & Sons, 1985.

In Brief:

The purpose of this book is to create an awareness of, or sensitivity to, behavior when one is traveling outside the United States or dealing with a visitor from overseas. An appreciation for and an understanding of cultural differences can prevent embarrassment, unhappiness and failure for the international business person. This guide to international behavior is presented in an enjoyable, easy-to-read, humorous manner.

The Economist Business Traveller's Guides
Prentice-Hall Press, 1987.

In Brief:

There are four separate books under this title for the following countries or regions: United Kingdom, Middle East, Japan and the United States. Each has sections on the following subjects: business practices and etiquette, finance, politics, economics, industry, professions, hotels, restaurants, airports, taxis, trains, sightseeing, shopping, sports, local business services and resources, communications, planning and reference, maps and charts.

Gender in International Relations
By J. Ann Tickner. Columbia University Press, 1992.

In Brief:

Demonstrating how a feminist perspective on international relations changes and expands our view of the global system, Ms. Tickner examines gender differences in the political, military, economic and ecological arenas.

Going International: How to Make Friends and Deal Effectively in the Global Marketplace
By Lennie Copeland and Lewis Griggs. Random House, 1985.

In Brief:

Going International is a guide for the international business person on how to make friends, win deals, manage people, market products and generally get things done in a foreign country.

International Business Handbook
Edited by V. H. (Manek) Kirpalani. Hawthorne Press, 1990.

In Brief:

This book is a practical guide for people interested in international business. It discusses several important aspects of international business including economics, politics, technology and law on a global level, and it offers an analysis of various issues and their influence on the international market.

International Business Studies: An Overview
Edited by Peter J. Buckley and Michael Z. Brooke. Blackwell, 1992.

In Brief:

This book provides a comprehensive survey that should be useful to specialists, researchers and students in international business and international marketing. It draws together studies and research done in many countries.

The International Businesswoman: A Guide to Success in the Global Marketplace
By Marlene L. Rossman. Praeger, 1986.

In Brief:

This book offers chapters on preparing for a career in international business, international negotiating, breaking down barriers, global marketing, life on the road, career and family, and how women can conduct business in different regions of the world.

International Careers
By Arthur H. Bell. Bob Adams Inc., 1990.

In Brief:

Written by a professional lecturer at Georgetown University's School of Business Administration, this book provides a six-step method for landing a job overseas, including employer listings for corporate jobs, government jobs and nonprofit jobs.

The book's reference section offers detailed information on U.S. firms that employ people internationally, foreign employers, foreign embassies in the U.S. and temporary overseas employment opportunities.

International Dimensions of Organizational Behavior
By Nancy J. Adler. PWS-KENT Publishing Company, 1991.

In Brief:

There is a shortage of textbooks available on the international dimensions of business. Nancy Adler, professor of organizational behavior and cross-cultural management at the Faculty of Management, McGill University, challenges readers to go beyond a parochialism and to see the world in global terms. This business textbook breaks down the conceptual, theoretical and practical boundaries that limit our ability to understand and manage people in countries worldwide.

The Knowledge Link: How Firms Compete Through Strategic Alliances
By Joseph L. Badaracco, Jr. Harvard Business School Press, 1991.

In Brief:

Today's corporations are entering strategic alliances to capitalize on two types of knowledge: migratory knowledge—which can be easily transferred between people or organizations in a formula or product—and embedded knowledge—which defines how a particular company does business. In today's business environment, companies need to utilize each type of knowledge to sustain their competitive advantage. Managing these alliances effectively will be a major factor in determining corporate success in the years ahead.

Losing Time: The Industrial Policy Debate
By Otis L. Graham, Jr. Harvard University Press, 1992.

In Brief:

This is a clear, lively, critical and fairly comprehensive account of the American debate about industrial policy in the 1980s. Much space is given to the economic conditions of that decade, the literature of American decline and summaries of the views of those who were for or against one kind of industrial policy or another. This enlightening book ends with some sensible proposals on how to improve America's future handling of this inescapable policy necessity.

Making Global Deals
By Jeswald W. Salacuse.

In Brief:

This is an indispensable tool that provides know-how and expert strategies for pinning down the international deal. Written by Jeswald Salacuse, dean and professor of international law at Tufts University, this book emphasizes the importance of preparation and provides checklists and ground rules for staying on top in negotiations. He explains how to overcome the obstacles and draw on the differences that may arise whether you are signing a multi-million-dollar contract or conducting a simple transaction.

A Manager's Guide to Globalization
By Stephen H. Rhinesmith. Business One Irwin/ASTD, 1993.

In Brief:

Drawing from the literature in business, comparative management, psychology, sociology, anthropology, philosophy and intercultural relations, Dr. Rhinesmith analyzes the factors which are key to management success in a constantly changing international market.

Managing Across Borders
By Christopher A. Bartlett and Sumantra Ghoshal.

In Brief:

Bartlett, a Harvard Business School professor, and Ghoshal, an associate professor at INSEAD, argue that in an environment of increasing complexity, diversity and change, companies cannot manage through structures that are one dimensional, symmetrical and static.

This book is the result of a five-year research project involving interviews with 236 managers in the United States, Japan and Europe. For large and small firms alike, it presents examples of and solutions to the problems encountered by companies operating businesses across borders.

Managing Cultural Differences
By Philip R. Harris and Robert T. Moran. Gulf Publishing Company, 1991.

In Brief:

This revised (third) edition contains significant new material, providing ideas and insights to broaden a manager's horizons and practical means for improving performance within or across national borders. The authors reveal specific cultural aspects for doing business in six regions of the world.

Mass Customization
By B. Joseph Pine, Harvard Business School Press, 1993.

In Brief:

The mass production of standardized goods was the source of America's economic strength for generations and became the model for successful industries. Today, that model is a major cause of the nation's declining competitiveness. Innovative companies are embracing a new paradigm of management—mass customization—that allows them to create greater variety and customization in their products and services at competitive prices, or better.

Companies that are leading their industries to this new frontier include McGraw-Hill, which can deliver custom-made classroom textbooks in quantities of one hundred or less; Motorola, which can manufacture any one of 29 million variations of pagers twenty minutes after it receives the order; and TWA Gateway Vacations, which can custom-design tour packages for what others charge for standard tours.

Joe Pine is a program manager for the IBM Corporation, where he has developed programs for implementing the principles of mass customization.

Rebuilding America's Work Force: Business Strategies to Close the Competitive Gap
By William H. Kilberg and Forster C. Smith. Business One Irwin, 1992.

In Brief:

The United States has been losing its competitive edge among industrialized countries, and a shortage of well-educated and trainable employees looms large. New ways of training employees are needed that go beyond outmoded assembly-line management techniques and instead enhance creativity and efficiency. This book provides case studies and practical techniques for enhancing employee performance.

Scanning the Future: A Long-Term Scenario Study of the World Economy, 1990–2015
By the Central Planning Bureau of The Netherlands. The Hauge: Sdu Publishers Plantijnstraat, 1992.

In Brief:

The long-established and respected Central Planning Bureau of The Netherlands presents its most ambitious study of the future of the world economy. Not surprisingly, skill and caution keep the authors from committing themselves to a single forecast, but there are many interesting hypotheses and suggestions about the shaping of national policies. There are some pervasive developments that, while hardly novel, are noteworthy because they turn up in almost all scenarios. Among them are "the further rise of East Asia, the long period of time needed to reconstruct East European economies, the spread of environmental problems and the risk of the emergence of antagonistic trading blocs."

Trend Tracking: The System to Profit from Today's Trends
By Stan Davis and Bill Davidson. Fireside/Simon & Schuster, 1991, 223 pages.

In Brief:

This book by two trend watchers provides easy-to-use guidelines for setting up a trend-tracking system using newspapers, magazines and other readily available sources.

Workplace 2000: The Revolution Reshaping American Business
By Joseph H. Boyett and Henry P. Conn. Plume, 1991.

In Brief:

This survival manual for tomorrow's uncertain future shows managers how to thrive in a workplace that operates at hyperspeed around the clock, with no supervisors, no job classifications, no definite work assignments and no defects in production or complaints from consumers.

SECTION B—DIRECTORIES

European Business Services Directory
Edited by Michael B. Huellmantel. Gale Research, 1992.

In Brief:

All kinds of European business firms are profiled in this directory, including advertising, computer services, technical services, financial and management. This is for the business person and international job seeker.

Export Programs: A Business Directory of U.S. Government Sources
Department of Commerce
Washington, D.C. 20230
Phone: (800) 833-8723
Fax: (202) 482-4473

In Brief:

The *Export Programs: A Business Directory of U.S. Government Sources* provides the reader with an overview of U.S. Government export assistance programs and contact points for further information and expertise in utilizing these programs. It offers information regarding agencies that can assist you with your international trading needs.

International Trade Directory of Contacts/Sources/Services
Hilary House, 1992.

In Brief:

The person looking for importers/exporters, firms with overseas employment opportunities, foreign firms in the United States, and other such useful information will find this directory especially helpful.

This massive four-volume directory lists more than 100,000 companies—large, medium-sized and small, in 190 countries—giving pertinent information on each. Volumes 1 to 3 list companies by country, from Afghanistan to Zimbabwe. Volume 4 organizes companies by the following indices: product, industry and alphabetical indices.

Worldwide Government Directory
Belmont Publications
1454 Belmont Street, NW
Washington, DC 20009
Phone: (800) 332-3535 or (202) 232-6334
Fax: (202) 462-5478

In Brief:

The *Worldwide Government Directory* (WGD) is a single-volume, 1,200 page reference guide to virtually every key elected and appointed government official in 192 nations—including all former Soviet Republics.

Now in its 9th edition, WGD provides over 50,000 names, office addresses, telephone, facsimile and cable numbers—up to 19 pages of information per country. Included are ministers, undersecretaries, directors, deputies, advisors, aides and other primary figures in the executive, legislative, judicial and diplomatic communities.

Key Officers of Foreign Service Posts—Guide for Business Representatives
Superintendent of Documents
U.S. Government Printing Office
Washington, D.C. 20402

In Brief:

This little handbook is one of the most valuable tools you will ever find. Compiled by the State Department, available for sale (ask for Publication #7877), and released in January 1983, the guide contains names, addresses and telephone numbers of all commercial officers, chiefs of missions, financial attachés, political officers, labor officers, consular officers, regional security officers, scientific attachés, agricultural officers and cultural affairs specialists in countries worldwide. It also lists U.S. Department of Commerce district offices throughout this country.

World Chamber of Commerce Directory
P.O. Box 1029
Loveland, CO 80539
Phone: (303) 663-3231
Fax: (303) 663-6187

In Brief:

This directory lists U.S. Chambers of Commerce, Economic Development Organizations, American Chambers of Commerce Abroad, Foreign Tourist Information Bureaus, Foreign Embassies in the United States, United States Embassies throughout the world and Foreign Chambers of Commerce in 146 countries.

World Trade Centers Association World Business Directory
Edited by Meghan A. O'Meara and Kimberley A. Peterson. Gale Research, 1992.

SECTION C—INTERNATIONAL BUSINESS ORGANIZATIONS

Association for Corporate Growth (ACG)
5700 Old Orchard Road, First Floor
Skokie, IL 60077-1057
Phone: (708) 966-1777

In Brief:

The Association for Corporate Growth was founded in 1954. Their mission is to train leaders who play a role in strategic corporate growth. ACG is a nonprofit organization which can help its members in the following areas:

○ Holding monthly (regional) chapter meetings along with seminars and conferences.

○ Reporting new techniques of corporate acquisitions and other up-to-date practices for both internal and international business development.

○ Publishing and sending the *Journal for Corporate Growth* three times per year.

○ Cosponsoring periodical conferences in Europe to foster awareness and understanding of international business trends.

The Conference Board
845 Third Avenue
New York, NY 10022-6601
Phone: (212) 759-0900
Fax: (212) 980-7014

The Conference Board Europe
Avenue Louise, 207-Bte 5, B-1050
Brussels, Belgium
Phone: 02-640-6240
Fax: 02-640-6735

The Conference Board of Canada
255 Smyth Road
Ottawa, Ontario, K1H-8M7
Phone: (613) 526-3280
Fax: (613) 526-4857

In Brief:

Founded in 1916, the Conference Board's twofold purpose is to improve the business enterprise system and to enhance the contribution of business to society.

To accomplish this, The Conference Board strives to be the leading global business membership organization that enables senior executives from all industries to explore and exchange ideas of impact on business policy and practices. To support this activity, The Conference Board provides a variety of forums and a professionally managed research program that identifies and reports objectively on key areas of changing management concern, opportunity and action. The Conference Board offers its members the following:

○ Access to published research materials.

○ National and international conferences on a variety of management topics.

Business Council for International Understanding

420 Lexington Avenue
New York, NY 10170
Phone: (212) 490-0460
Fax: (212) 697-8526

In Brief:

The Business Council for International Understanding's New York headquarters works with the United States Department of State, Department of Commerce and other government departments in arranging consultations with industry executives for U.S. ambassadors and senior embassy counselors. The BCIU cooperates with U.S. and foreign governments on problems of democratic, economic and social developments by organizing small discussion groups for heads of state, their ministries and foreign industry missions.

International Society for Intercultural Education, Training and Research

1414 22nd Street, NW
Washington, D.C. 20037

In Brief:

The International Society for Intercultural Education, Training and Research is a professional association of cross-cultural trainers, personnel administrators, academics and others interested in intercultural education. The organization sponsors an annual conference and other events, and publishes books in this field.

Committee on Changing International Realities

c/o National Planning Association
1424 16th Street, NW, Suite 700
Washington, D.C. 20036
Phone: (202) 265-7685

In Brief:

The Committee on Changing International Realities analyzes major international political and economic changes that affect the United States' private sector, with emphasis on the implications for U.S. economic competitiveness and relations with developing nations. It researches topics such as productivity, innovation, and research and development.

Council for International Business Risk Management

P.O. Box 811765
Dallas, Texas 75381
Phone: (214) 352-5801
Fax: (214) 350-7609

In Brief:

The Council for International Business Risk Management provides a forum for communication and exchange among members and analysts in other fields. Its members are individuals and institutions concerned with the need for timely information and analysis on national, international and government policy issues and their implications on international business.

International Association for Business Organizations

P.O. Box 30149
Baltimore, Maryland 21270
Phone: (301) 581-1373

In Brief:

The International Association for Business Organizations grants charters for international and national and business organizations. It conducts market studies, supplies member organizations with management assistance and encourages joint marketing services and international trade assistance among members.

International Council for Small Business

c/o Institute of Entrepreneurial Studies
St. Louis University
3674 Lindell Boulevard
St. Louis, Missouri 63108

In Brief:

The International Council for Small Business consists of management educators, researchers, government officials and professionals in fifty countries. It fosters discussion of topics pertaining to the development and improvement of small business management.

National Council of World Affairs Organization

1726 M Street, NW #800
Washington, D.C. 20036
Phone: (202) 785-4703
Fax: (202) 833-2369

In Brief:

The National Council of World Affairs is dedicated to a singular concept: that of seeing the world from a different viewpoint—through the eyes of informed, stimulating guest speakers, through lively discussion and through travel abroad. There are 38 chapters throughout the United States providing a forum for education on international issues, including foreign policy and international economic issues.

Organization of Women in International Trade (OWIT)

1992 President: Dorothy Schumacher
Phone: (708) 595-2840

In Brief:

The Organization of Women in International Trade (OWIT) is a nonprofit organization dedicated to "serving the professional needs of persons engaged in international trade." OWIT is a grass roots organization and serves as an umbrella for fourteen independent chapters throughout the United States and affiliate relationships in Moscow, Tokyo, Egypt and Mexico. OWIT can offer its members:

○ Monthly chapter meetings featuring speakers on international business topics relevant to the region.

○ Opportunities to attend international conferences and trade missions.

○ An international directory which is distributed to members worldwide.

United States Council for International Business

1212 Avenue of the Americas
New York, New York 10036
Phone: (212) 354-4480

In Brief:

The United States Council for International Business serves as the U.S. National Committee of the International Chamber of Commerce. It enables multinational enterprises to operate effectively by representing their interests to intergovernmental and governmental bodies and by keeping enterprises advised of international developments having a major impact on their operations.

World Trade Centers Association

In Brief:

The World Trade Center (WTC) Association is an organization comprised of 115 member groups in almost fifty nations. Founded in 1968, the purpose of the association is to encourage the expansion of world trade and to promote international business relationships. A world trade center concept brings together business and government agencies involved in foreign trade. A world trade center puts all services associated with international trade under one roof. The world trade center in any city is a business "shopping center," complementing and supporting the existing services of private business and government agencies. You can use a WTC to:

○ Receive information about business opportunities.

○ Meet influential foreign business people.

○ Broaden your horizon with regard to career possibilities available internationally.

The following is a list of World Trade Centers in cities around the United States:

Atlanta
World Trade Club of Atlanta, Inc.
240 Peachtree Street, Suite 220
Atlanta, GA 30303
Phone: (404) 525-4144

Baltimore
The World Trade Center Baltimore
Baltimore, MD 21202
Phone: (301) 659-4544

Baltimore
The Merchants Club
206 East Redwood Street
Baltimore, MD 21202
Phone: (310) 742-6467

Boston
International Business Center
  of New England
22 Batterymarch Street
Boston, MA 02210
Phone: (617) 542-0426

Chicago
Club International
The Drake Hotel
140 East Walton Place
Chicago, IL 60611
Phone: (312) 787-2200

Colorado Springs
Rocky Mountain World Trade Center
Red Rock Canyon Project
3221 West Colorado Avenue
Colorado Springs, CO 80904
Phone: (303) 633-9041

Columbus
World Trade and Technology Center
  of Columbus
10793 State Route 37 West
Sunbury, OH 43074
Phone: (614) 965-2974

Des Moines
Iowa World Trade Center Des Moines
3200 Ruan Center
666 Grand Avenue
Des Moines, IA 50390
Phone: (515) 245-2555

Ft. Lauderdale
World Trade Center Fort Lauderdale,
  Florida
P.O. Box 13066
1800 Eller Drive
Port Everglades, FL 33316
Phone: (305) 523-5307

Greensboro
World Trade Center—North Carolina
P.O. Box 19290
Greensboro, NC 27419

Honolulu
Hawaii International Services Branch
Department of Planning and
    Economic Development
P.O. Box 2359
Honolulu, HI 96804
Phone: (808) 548-3048

Houston
World Trade Center Houston
1520 Texas Avenue, Suites 1D and 1E
Houston, TX 77002
Phone: (713) 225-0968

Jacksonville
Jacksonville International Trade
Association
Jacksonville Chamber of Commerce
3 Independence Drive
P.O. Box 329
Jacksonville, FL 32201
Phone: (904) 353-0300

Long Beach
The Port of Long Beach
925 Harbor Plaza
P.O. Box 570
Long Beach, CA 92801
Phone: (213) 437-0041

Miami
Execucentre International
444 Brickell Avenue, Suite 650
Miami, FL 33131
Phone: (305) 374-8300

New Orleans
International House—WTC
611 Gravier Street
New Orleans, LA 70230
Phone: (504) 522-3591

New York
World Trade Center New York
The Port Authority of New York and
    New Jersey
1 World Trade Center, Suite 63 West
New York, NY 10048
Phone: (212) 466-8380

Norfolk
World Trade Center Norfolk
600 World Trade Center
Norfolk, VA 23510
Phone: (804) 623-8000

Orlando
World Trade Center Orlando
P.O. Box 1234
Orlando, FL 32801
Phone: (305) 425-1234

Pomona
Inland Pacific World Trade Institute
422 West Seventh Street, Suite 302
Los Angeles, CA 90014
Phone: (213) 627-6738

Portland
Columbia World Trade Center
   Corporation
121 West Salmon
Portland, OR 97204
Phone: (503) 220-3067

San Francisco
World Trade Center of San Francisco,
   Inc.
1170 Sacramento Street, Penthouse B
San Francisco, CA 92108
Phone: (415) 928-3438

Santa Ana
World Trade Center Association of
   Orange County
200 East Sandpointe Avenue
Santa Ana, CA 92707
Phone: (714) 549-8151

Sarasota
World Trade Council of Southwest
   Florida
P.O. Box 911
Sarasota, FL 33578
Phone: (813) 366-4060

Seattle
Seattle World Trade Center
Corporation
500 Union Street, Suite 840
Seattle, WA 96101
Phone: (206) 622-4121

St. Paul
Minnesota World Trade Center
1300 Conwed Tower
444 Cedar Street
St. Paul, MN 55101
Phone: (612) 297-1580

Tacoma
World Trade Center Tacoma
P.O. Box 1837
Tacoma, WA 96401
Phone: (206) 383-5841, Ext. 321

Tampa
Tampa Bay International Trade
   Council
P.O. Box 420
Tampa, FL 33601
Phone: (813) 228-7777, Ext. 234

Toledo
Toledo World Trade Center
136 North Summit Street
P.O. Box 2087
Toledo, OH 43603
Phone: (4193) 255-7226

Washington, D.C.
World Trade Center Washington
1000 Connecticut Avenue, NW, Ste. 707
Washington, DC 20036
Phone: (202) 955-6164

SECTION D—UNITED STATES GOVERNMENT SERVICES AND AGENCIES

Bureau of Census, Department of Commerce
Washington, D.C. 20230
Phone: (301) 763-7662

In Brief:

The Bureau of Census is the statistical gathering agency of the Federal Government. Regarding international trade, the bureau tracks export and import statistics.

Bureau of Export Administration (BXA): Department of Commerce
14th Street and Pennsylvania Avenue, NW, Room 1099
Washington, D.C. 20230
Phone: (202) 482-8536
Fax: (202) 482-3322

In Brief:

The Bureau of Export Administration can help you in the following areas:

- Help with all of your export licensing needs.

- Offer regulatory updates (free) through the *OEL Insider.*

- Help in the process of requesting an Export Commodity Control Number (ECCN).

Export-Import Bank (EXIMBANK)
811 Vermont Ave., N.W.
Washington, D.C. 20571
Phone: (202) 566-2117
Fax: (202) 566-7524

In Brief:

The Export-Import Bank, commonly known as EXIMBANK, is an independent corporate agency of the U.S. Government chartered by Congress.

EXIMBANK's mission is to "facilitate export financing of U.S. goods and services by neutralizing the effect of export credit subsidies from other governments and by absorbing reasonable credit risks that are beyond the current reach of the private sector." EXIMBANK may assist you in the following ways:

○ Helping small companies to get pre-export financing from commercial lenders with a 90 percent guarantee of principal.

○ Offering loan and guarantee programs up to 85 percent of U.S. export value with competitive, fixed interest rate financing.

○ Providing guarantees to provide repayment protection for creditworthy buyers of U.S. goods and services exports.

○ Guaranteeing payments on crossborder or international leases structured as either operating or finance leasing.

○ Offering export credit insurance for exporters and commercial lenders.

International Economic Policy (IEP)

Department of Commerce
Washington, D.C. 20230
IEP individual country desk officer information: (202) 482-3022

In Brief:

The International Economic Policy (IEP) consists of an officer for every country in the world. IEP desk officers can help you in the following areas:

○ Advising you on the trade opportunities possible for your product in individual countries.

○ Offering specific information to help an exporter assess the political, social and economic climate in a particular country of interest.

International Trade Administration (ITA): United States Department of Commerce

Department of Commerce
Washington, D.C. 20230
Phone: (800) 833-8723
Fax: (202) 482-4473

In Brief:

The International Trade Administration (ITA) was established in 1980 to promote world trade and strengthen the international trade and investment position of the United States. ITA is a subsidiary of the U.S. Department of Commerce and is responsible for nonagricultural trade operations of the U.S. Government and promoting trade policy negotiations of U.S. trade representatives.

The four divisions of the ITA include International Economic Policy (IEP), which maintains in-depth information on trade and investment issues in countries around the world; Import Administration (IA), which develops policies pertaining to trade and investment; Trade Development (TD), which provides information on the competitive strengths of U.S. industries in domestic and international markets; and the U.S. Foreign and Commercial Service (USFCS), which offers services geared to meet the needs of the U.S. exporting and international business community.

The Department of Commerce publishes vast amounts of statistical data and descriptive market analysis, available in a number of reports, including Export Statistics Profiles, TOP Bulletin, International Market Research Reports, Country Market Surveys, Annual Worldwide Industry Review, World Traders Data Reports, Overseas Export Promotion Calendar, and more. The Department's biweekly magazine, *Business America,* includes news and opportunities in international business.

Overseas Private Investment Corporation (OPIC)

1100 New York Avenue, NW
Washington, D.C. 20527
Phone: (800) 424-OPIC
Finance Department Fax: (202) 408-9866

In Brief:

The Overseas Private Investment Corporation (OPIC) is a Federal Government agency whose goal is to promote economic growth in developing countries by encouraging American private investment in those countries. OPIC offers programs in investment finance, investor service and investment insurance. Specifically, OPIC can help overseas investors by:

    ○ Providing small and medium-sized firms with a "Small Business Insurance Package" deal.

○ Providing insurance coverage overseas in case of expropriation, currency inconvertibility or political violence.

Trade Assistance Planning Office

USDA/FAS
3101 Park Center Drive, Suite 1103
Alexandria, VA 22302
Phone: (703) 305-2771
Fax: (703) 305-2788

In Brief:

The Trade Assistance and Planning Office serves agricultural exporters by:

○ Providing information and assistance to persons interested in export programs carried out by the Foreign Agricultural Service and the Commodity Credit Corporation.

○ Helping get information on export-related programs managed by other Federal agencies.

○ Serving as a contact point for minority and small businesses needing assistance in exporting agricultural products.

○ Helping U.S. agricultural exporters contact the appropriate Federal agency administering trade remedy laws.

○ Arranging for speakers on a variety of agricultural trade issues.

Trade Development (TD), Department of Commerce

Department of Commerce
Washington, D.C. 20230
Phone: (202) 377-1461
Fax: (202) 377-5697

In Brief:

The Trade Development specialists work with representatives of manufacturing and service industries to identify trade opportunities and obstacles by product or service, industry sector and market. They conduct executive trade missions, trade fairs, marketing seminars and business counseling to assist U.S. businesses in their export efforts. In addition TD desk officers can help you with the following:

○ Offer information on the market prospects for exportable goods from abrasive products to yogurt.

Trade Information Center: United States Department of Commerce

Department of Commerce
Washington, D.C. 20230
Phone: (800) 833-8723
Fax: (202) 482-4473

In Brief:

The Trade Information Center is a one-step information source on the multitude of Federal export assistance programs available. International trade specialists can be reached weekdays from 8:30 A.M. to 6:00 P.M. on the center's toll-free "800" line. A message center takes calls after hours.

Trade Remedy Assistance Office (TRAO), International Trade Commission (ITC)

500 E Street, SW
Washington, D.C. 20436
Phone: (202) 205-2000

In Brief:

The International Trade Commission (ITC) is an independent and bipartisan agency whose major task is to make determinations of injury and threat of injury to U.S. industry by reason of imports. It is the government's "think tank" on international trade. Of particular interest to import/exporters is the Trade Remedy Assistance Office (TRAO) which was established to offer assistance to businesses seeking benefits or relief under U.S. trade laws.

United States Agency for International Development Center for Trade and Investment Services

Washington, D.C. 20523-0229
Phone: (800) USAID-4-U
Fax: (202) 663-2670

In Brief:

The Center for Trade and Investment Services (CTIS) is the central information and referral service for AID—the U.S. agency for international development. CTIS promotes linkages between private sectors in the United States and foreign entrepreneurs in developing nations. CTIS can help you in the following areas:

○ Serving as a central point of contact for all inquiries about business opportunities in USAID-assisted countries.

○ Analyzing company needs to identify specific information requirements or giving referrals to other organizations when necessary.

○ Providing information about USAID's financed procurement opportunities.

○ Linking U.S. firms with entrepreneurs overseas.

○ Sponsoring industry-specific conferences.

United States and Foreign Commercial Service District Offices

In Brief:

The domestic offices of the Department of Commerce have trade specialists who counsel small and medium-sized manufacturers, helping them export United States goods. This excellent resource offers assistance in assessing your export potential, selecting export markets, strategies and selling techniques.

ALABAMA
Birmingham, 35205
Berry Building
2015 Second Avenue, North
Phone: (205) 731-1331

ALASKA
Anchorage, 99508
World Trade Center
4201 Tudor Center Drive, Suite 319
Phone: (907) 271-6237

ARIZONA
Phoenix, 85012
Phoenix Plaza
2901 North Central Avenue
Phone: (602) 640-2513

ARKANSAS
Little Rock, 72201
425 West Capitol Avenue, 7th Floor
Phone: (501) 324-5794

CALIFORNIA
Los Angeles, 90024
11000 Wilshire Boulevard, Room 800
Phone: (310) 575-7105

*Newport Beach, 92660-3198
3300 Irvine Avenue, Suite 305
Phone: (714) 660-1688

San Diego, 92122
6363 Greenwich Drive, Suite 230
Phone: (619) 557-5395

San Francisco, 94104
250 Montgomery Street, 14th Floor
Phone: (415) 705-2300

Santa Clara, 95054-1127
5201 Great American Parkway, Ste. 333
Phone: (408) 291-7625

COLORADO
Denver, 80202
1625 Broadway, Suite 680
Phone: (303) 844-6622

CONNECTICUT
Hartford, 06103
Federal Building, Room 610-B
450 Main Street
Phone: (203) 240-3530

DELAWARE
Serviced by Philadelphia District Office

DISTRICT OF COLUMBIA
Serviced by Gaithersburg, Maryland
    Branch Office

FLORIDA
*Clearwater, 34615
128 North Osceola Avenue
Phone: (813) 461-0011

Miami, 33130
Federal Building, Suite 224
51 South West First Avenue
Phone: (305) 350-5267

*Orlando, 32801
Eola Park Centre
200 East Robinson Street, Suite 695
Phone: (407) 648-6235

*Tallahassee, 32399-2000
Collins Building
107 West Gaines Street
Phone: (904) 488-6469

GEORGIA
Atlanta, 30341
Plaza Square North
4360 Chamblee Dunwoody Road
Phone: (404) 452-9101

Savannah, 31401
120 Barnard Street, A-107
Phone: (912) 652-4204

HAWAII
Honolulu, 96850
400 Ala Moana Boulevard, Room 4106
P.O. Box 50026
Phone: (808) 546-8694

*Denotes Trade Specialist at a Branch Office.

IDAHO
Boise, 83720
Joe R. Williams Building
700 West State Street, 2nd Floor
Phone: (208) 334-4450

ILLINOIS
Chicago, 60603
Mid-Continental Plaza Building
55 East Monroe Street, Room 1406
Phone: (312) 353-4450

*Rockford, 61110-0247
515 North Court Street
P.O. Box 1747
Phone: (815) 987-4347

*Wheaton, 60187
Illinois Institute of Technology
201 East Loop Road
Phone: (312) 353-4332

INDIANA
(Indianapolis) Carmel, 46032
Penwood One
11405 North Pennsylvania Street,
   Suite 106
Phone: (317) 582-2300

IOWA
Des Moines, 50309
817 Federal Building
210 Walnut Street
Phone: (515) 284-4222

KANSAS
*Wichita, 67214-4695
151 North Volutsia
Phone: (316) 269-6160

KENTUCKY
Louisville, 40202
Gene Snyder Courthouse and
   Customhouse Building
601 West Broadway, Room 636B
Phone: (502) 582-5066

LOUISIANA
New Orleans, 70130
432 World Trade Center
2 Canal Street
Phone: (504) 589-6546

MAINE
*Augusta, 04330
77 Sewall Street
Phone: (207) 622-8249

MARYLAND
Baltimore, 21202
413 U.S. Customhouse
40 South Gay Street
Phone: (301) 962-3560

MASSACHUSETTS
Boston, 02210
World Trade Center
Commonwealth Pier Area, Suite 307
Phone: (617) 565-8563

MICHIGAN
Detroit, 48226
1140 McNamara Building
447 Michigan Avenue
Phone: (313) 226-3650

*Grand Rapids, 49503
300 Monroe, North West
Phone: (616) 456-2411

*Denotes Trade Specialist at a Branch Office.

MINNESOTA
Minneapolis, 55401
108 Federal Building
110 South 4th Street
Phone: (612) 349-1638

MISSISSIPPI
Jackson, 39213-2005
201 West Capital Street, Suite 310
Phone: (601) 960-4388

MISSOURI
Kansas City, 64106
601 East 12th Street, Room 635
Phone: (816) 426-3141

St. Louis, 63105
8182 Maryland Avenue, Suite 303
Phone: (314) 425-3302

MONTANA
Served by Portland District Office

NEBRASKA
Omaha, 68137
11133 "O" Street
Phone: (402) 221-3664

NEVADA
Reno, 89502
1755 East Plumb Lane, Room 152
Phone: (702) 784-5203

NEW HAMPSHIRE
*Portsmith (Boston District), 03302
601 Spaulding Turnpike, Suite 29
Phone: (603) 334-6074

NEW JERSEY
Trenton, 08648
3131 Princeton Pike, Building 6,
   Suite 100
Phone: (609) 989-2100

NEW MEXICO
Albuquerque (Dallas District), 87106
851 University Boulevard, South East,
   #203
Phone: (505) 246-6205

NEW YORK
Buffalo, 14202
1312 Federal Building
111 West Huron Street
Phone: (716) 846-4191

New York, 10278
Federal Office Building,
26 Federal Plaza, Room 3718
Phone: (212) 264-0634

*Rochester, 14604
111 East Avenue, Suite 220
Phone: (716) 264-0634

NORTH CAROLINA
Greensboro, 27401
400 West Market Street, Suite 400
Phone: (919) 333-5345

NORTH DAKOTA
Serviced by Omaha District Office

*Denotes Trade Specialist at a Branch Office.

OHIO
Cincinnati, 45202
9504 Federal Building
550 Main Street
Phone: (513) 684-2944

Cleveland, Ohio 44114
668 Eudlid Avenue
Phone: (216) 522-4750

OKLAHOMA
Oklahoma City, 73116
6601 Broadway Extension
Phone: (405) 231-5302

*Tulsa, 74127
440 South Houston Street
Phone: (918) 581-7650

OREGON
Portland, 97204
One World Trade Center
121 South West Salmon Street
Phone: (503) 326-3001

PENNSYLVANIA
(Philadelphia) King of Prussia, 19406
660 American Avenue, Suite 201
Phone: (215) 962-4980

Pittsburgh, 15222
2002 Federal Building
1000 Liberty Avenue
Phone: (412) 644-2850

PUERTO RICO
San Juan (Hato Rey), 00918
Federal Building
Chardon Avenue, Room 659
Phone: (809) 766-4555

RHODE ISLAND
*Providence (Hartford District Office),
  02903
7 Jackson Walkway
Phone: (401) 528-5104

SOUTH CAROLINA
Columbia, 29201
Strom Thurmond Federal Building
1835 Assembly Street, Suite 172
Phone: (803) 765-5345

*Charleston, 29424
JC Long Building
9 Liberty Street, Room 128
Phone: (803) 727-4361

SOUTH DAKOTA
Serviced by Omaha District Office

TENNESSEE
Nashville, 37219-1505
Parkway Towers
404 James Robertson Parkway,
  Suite 114
Phone: (615) 736-5161

*Knoxville, 37915
301 East Church Avenue
Phone: (615) 545-4367

*Memphis, 38103
The Falls Building
22 North Front Street, Suite 200
Phone: (901) 544-4137

*Denotes Trade Specialist at a Branch Office.

TEXAS
*Austin, 78701
410 East 5th Street, Suite 320A
Phone: (512) 482-5939

Dallas, 75242-0787
World Trade Center
2050 North Stemmons Freeway,
    Suite 170
Phone: (214) 767-0542

Houston, 77002
#1 Allen Center
500 Dallas, Suite 1160
Phone: (713) 229-2578

UTAH
Salt Lake City, 84111
324 South State Street, Suite 105
Phone: (801) 524-5116

VERMONT
Serviced by Boston District Office

VIRGINIA
Richmond, 232340
8010 Federal Building
400 North 8th Street
Phone: (804) 771-2246

WASHINGTON
Seattle, 98121
3131 Elliott Avenue, Suite 290
Phone: (206) 553-5615

WEST VIRGINIA
Charleston, 25301
405 Capital Street, Suite 807
Phone: (304) 347-5123

WISCONSIN
Milwaukee, 53202
517 East Wisconsin Avenue, Room 596
Phone: (414) 297-3473

WYOMING
Serviced by Denver District Office

United States Customs Services, Department of the Treasury
1301 Constitution Avenue, NW
Washington, D.C. 20229

In Brief:

The major responsibility of the U.S. Customs Service, as reported in the guide *Importing into the United States,* is "to administer the tariff act of 1930." Their duties include the assessment and collection of all duties, fees and taxes on imported merchandise. Moreover, they enforce laws and treaties and combat smuggling and fraud on revenue. The U.S. Customs Service offers a pamphlet that answers general questions about importing, called *Importing Requirements.*

SECTION E - LANGUAGE INSTRUCTION

What most business people are looking for is language instruction that will give them quick, solid results in terms of practical, day-to-day language ability. You may be lucky enough to have such instruction offered at your local university or community college. (Check particularly with extended or continued education departments which offer many classes taught on weekends or in the evenings.)

The following is a short list of the headquarters of popular and effective language programs. By calling or writing these offices, you can find a language school in your area:

Berlitz Language Centers
1050 Connecticut Avenue
Washington, DC 20008
Phone: (202) 331-1160

Inlingua School of Languages
1030 15th Street, NW, Suite 828
Washington, DC 20005
Phone: (202) 289-8666

International Center for Language Studies
727 15th Street, NW, Suite 400
Washington, DC 20005
Phone: (202) 639-8800

Linguex
1255 23rd Street, Suite 285
Washington, DC 20005
Phone: (202) 296-1112

SECTION F—INTERNATIONAL EDUCATION, WORKSHOPS AND PROGRAMS

American Graduate School of International Management
Glendale, Arizona

In Brief:

The American Graduate School of International Management, also known as Thunderbird School, was founded in 1946 by a group of international-minded citizens led by a lieutenant general determined to solve the problem of innocents abroad who were not prepared for international assignments. In addition to stressing foreign language training, the school gives customized, concentrated programs embracing the whole spectrum of foreign culture shock. Cultural programs can be arranged for a few days up to weeks or months. Intensive language courses take six to eight weeks.

Business Council for International Understanding
The American University
Washington, D.C.

In Brief:

The Business Council for International Understanding (BCIU) educates and trains both Americans and foreign nationals to operate in other cultures. With over 25,000 graduates, from technicians to corporate C.E.O.s, in 143 countries, it is the oldest organization in the business. Eighty percent of the programs are conducted in Washington, 20 percent on-site or overseas. For each client company, programs can be custom-designed for corporate staffs; negotiating teams; adults, teenagers and children; reentering families; or foreign families coming to the U.S.

Programs run from one day to several weeks and include intercultural communication, area and country studies, and/or language training.

David M. Kennedy International Center

Brigham Young University
Box 61 FOB
Provo, UT 84602
Phone: (801) 378-6528

In Brief:

The David M. Kennedy International Center offers academic courses to aid intercultural understanding. Its publications include *Culturegrams*—a series of four-page leaflets covering 102 nations. Each pamphlet discusses the customs and courtesies of a country, describes the people and their life-style, and includes an overview of each nation and its government.

Other publications include *Infograms* on various subjects, such as "Questions Asked about America," "Coming Home Again," "Keeping the Law Internationally," "Jet Lag" and so on.

European Institute of Business Administration (INSEAD)

Fountainebleau Cedex, France

In Brief:

For more than 30 years, INSEAD's mission has been to prepare and develop executives for managing in an international environment. INSEAD offers a ten-month MBA program in general management, a Ph.D. program in management, and various executive education programs with a dual emphasis on general management and international perspective.

Kinsey Consulting Services

Carol Kinsey Goman, Ph.D.
P.O. Box 8255
Berkeley, California 94707
Phone: (510) 943-7850
Fax: (510) 524-9577

In Brief:

Carol Kinsey Goman, Ph.D., president of Kinsey Consulting Services, presents keynote speeches and seminars on a variety of business topics. She addresses national and international audiences at organization and association meetings. Her global business topics include:

- ○ *The Keys to Successful Global Management*
- ○ *The Role of the Global Communicator*
- ○ *Managing Organizational Change*

Monterey Institute of International Studies
Monterey, California

In Brief:

The Monterey Institute of International Studies, a language-based graduate school of international affairs which grants degrees in business as well as policy studies, formed a Center for Language Services. This unit provides highly trained, skilled interpreters and translators and, at the same time, provides teachers to educate people in small groups.

The school's in-house Training for Service Abroad program, which offers one-on-one training in up to forty languages, has provided language and culture training for people from many of the United States' largest businesses and for many representatives of the news media.

Pepperdine University
Malibu, CA

In Brief:

Pepperdine University began its Master in International Business program in 1989 because of demand from both students and corporations. Their goal is to "put out culturally sensitive graduates who hopefully can function in an international context without making the faux pas that some Americans are subject to." It takes twenty months of full-time work to earn an MIB degree, and students spend eight of those months in classes and corporate internships in

France or Germany. Pepperdine is now considering additional internships in the Far East and Spain.

The School for International Training
Brattleboro, Vermont

In Brief:

The School for International Training is the academic offshoot of the celebrated Experiment in International Living, founded in 1932. The school offers undergraduate and graduate degree programs in addition to short-term training for corporate executives. Courses are tailor-made to each participant's goals.

Transemantics, Inc.
4301 Connecticut Avenue, NW
Washington, D.C.

In Brief:

Transemantics maintains briefing and language centers in three capital locations and also sends trainers anywhere in the United States. Programs are tailored to particular needs and presented by an area expert and a cultural representative who can act out potential real-life problems with participants.

The institute also offers multilingual support from translating and interpreting to multilingual typesetting and editing, adaptation of promotional literature to foreign markets, film and tape narration and convention services.

U.S. Department of State, Foreign Service Institute, Overseas Briefing Center
1400 Key Boulevard
Arlington, Virginia 22209

In Brief:

The Overseas Briefing Center prepares State Department personnel for international assignments. It maintains a library which is not open to the public. However, if you are trying to establish a cross-cultural training or expatriate service for your organization, the Center staff will be happy to share its knowledge. It is a resource worth using. The State Department also produces in-depth country *Area Studies* and briefer *Post Reports* on virtually every country where there is a U.S. embassy. These are available at government bookstores throughout the country.

University of Miami
Miami, FL

In Brief:

At the University of Miami's School of Business Administration, a new Master of International Business Studies program combining an MBA with a Master of Science degree in International Business was launched in August of 1993. This two-year total immersion program (no part-timers are accepted) includes a four-month foreign corporate internship, fluency in a second language and various seminars that give students special knowledge and skills vital to doing business abroad.

University of South Carolina
Columbia, S.C.

In Brief:

Voted the best international business department in the country in 1990, 1991 and 1992 in surveys conducted by *U.S. News & World Report,* South Carolina's Master of International Business Studies (MIBS) was begun in 1974, and it was the first business school in the nation to require all students to be fluent in a second language, receive cross-cultural training and complete a six-month internship abroad with multinational companies. The school offers language classes in French, Italian, Spanish, Portuguese, German, Russian, Arabic, Japanese, Korean and Chinese.

Note: Today many other universities are offering—or soon will introduce—international programs that feature work internships abroad as well as language, business and area studies components. One fine example is UCLA's John E. Anderson Graduate School of Management, which established a separate international business center in 1989. The intensive 24-month certificate program combines language and area studies with the Anderson School's top-flight MBA program.

SECTION G—PAMPHLETS, TAPES, VIDEOS, ETC.

Background Notes
Superintendent of Documents
United States Government Printing Office
Washington, D.C. 20402

In Brief:

These factual information leaflets from the U.S. State Department are available for 157 countries and updated regularly. You can get them at many libraries or buy them directly from the U.S. Government Printing Office.

The Business Customs and Protocol Series
Stanford Research Institute International (SRI)
333 Ravenswood Avenue
Menlo Park, California 94025

In Brief:

This series of booklets has been produced for business people by SRI. They concentrate on how to get started, how to get things done and how to facilitate mutual understanding in international business.

Copeland Griggs Productions
411 15th Avenue
San Francisco, California 94118
Phone: (415) 668-4200

In Brief:

Copeland Griggs Productions has produced a series of films and videotapes called *Going International,* to help the American traveler become more effective in international business. Parts I and II focus on cultural differences in business. Parts III and IV deal with cultural shock and with unexpected difficulties that employees and families experience upon returning to the U.S. Parts V and VI are geared toward foreigners coming to the U.S. to live. Part VII offers tips on safe international travel.

Cultural Diversity—"At the Heart of Bull"
Bull HN Information Systems, Inc.

In Brief:

Originally developed by the Human Resources and Communication groups of Bull HN Information Systems, Inc., this video is designed to inform and assist people in dealing with ethnic and cultural diversity in the workplace. The video focuses specifically on cultural differences between French and Americans, as seen from the perspective of Bull employees. It is a candid, fast-paced look at how employees from both cultures perceive themselves, one another and the world around them.

Cultural Diversity—"At the Heart of Bull" is useful for any company that has employees or customers around the world. It is also being used in business school courses on global management. The video is distributed (for sale or one-week rental) by Intercultural Press.

The Intercultural Press, Inc.
P.O. Box 700
Yarmouth, Maine 04096
Phone: (207) 846-5168
Fax: (207) 846-5181

In Brief:

The Intercultural Press publishes an extensive list of titles about cross-cultural interaction and communication, including country-specific information. They also put out two popular series. One is titled *Update* and covers the topics of how to prepare to leave home, what to do upon arrival, local regulations and business practices, etc. The other series is called *Interacts* and analyzes how Americans do things differently from people of other cultures and how relationships are thus affected.

The International American
201 East 36th Street
New York, New York 10016

In Brief:

The International American is a monthly newsletter that addresses the interests and concerns of frequent business travelers and the expatriate community.

...tional Cultural Enterprises, Inc.
...tmouth Lane
...d, IL 60015
...none: (800) 626-2772 or (708) 945-9516
Fax: (708) 945-9614

In Brief:

"Doing Business Around the World" are international audio guides for 25 countries. They have been developed by International Cultural Enterprises in association with Stanford Research Institute International, one of the world's top business-consulting firms. Each audio guide covers a particular country and comes with a booklet of essential facts and information about the country, including:

○ How to make initial contacts

○ Negotiating skills

○ How to facilitate mutual understanding and agreement

○ Decision makers and decision making

○ Social contact and entertainment

○ Regional differences

Managing Across Borders

Harvard Business School Management Programs
Mail Box 230-5
Soldier Field
Boston, MA 02163

In Brief:

"Managing Across Borders" is a video-based program that explains the new global competitive environment and what corporate capabilities are needed now to succeed in this new environment. The program features interviews with executives at five major United States, European and Japanese companies: ABB Asea Brown Boveri, Ltd., Becton Dickinson and Company, Corning Inc., NEC Corporation and Unilever.

Researchers Christopher Bartlerr, at Harvard Business School, and Sumantra Ghoshal, now at INSEAD, looked at companies which were succeeding in spite of turmoil and found that three corporate skills are critical to success in the global arena:

○ The ability to respond to local needs and differences around the world.

○ The ability to achieve global economies of scale.

○ The ability to innovate anywhere in the world and to transfer that learning and innovation around the world quickly.

ABOUT THE AUTHOR

Carol Kinsey Goman, Ph.D., president of Kinsey Consulting Services, is an internationally recognized expert on the "human side" of organizational change. She has served as adjunct faculty for John F. Kennedy University in their international MBA program and for the Executive Education Department at the University of California in Berkeley. She is an instructor for the Chamber of Commerce of the United States at their Institutes for Leadership Development. Her published books include *Change-Busting: 50 Ways to Sabotage Organizational Change, Creativity in Business, The Loyalty Factor, Managing for Commitment,* and *Adapting to Change: Making It Work for You.*

Addressing conferences and conventions around the world, Carol's upbeat style has earned her a deserved reputation as one of America's best keynote speakers. Her programs are delivered to corporations and professional associations for clients that include: AT&T, Motorola, Westinghouse, Bank of America, DuPont, Kaiser Permanente, Federal Express, the American Chamber of Commerce in Hong Kong, The Conference Board in London, KF Group in Sweden, Bell Canada and the Puerto Rico Hotel and Tourism Association.

For more information on her books and programs, please contact:

Carol Kinsey Goman, Ph.D.
Kinsey Consulting Services
P.O. Box 8255
Berkeley, CA 94707
Phone (510) 943-7850
Fax (510) 524-9577